PRAISE FOR
INTERPRETATION TOOLKIT

"I have an entire shelf of books on dream interpretation and I've taken several courses on the topic, but none were useful for me. I just couldn't get to the root of what was going on in my dreams. *Dream Interpretation Toolkit* is the first book that makes sense. Sylvia provides the revelation and sound teaching necessary for me to see how the Holy Spirit speaks to me in my dreams. I consider this book to be a resource that I will use for the rest of my life."

—**Candace Lovell**, *Ft. Walton Beach, FL*

"Sylvia really hit a home run with *Dream Interpretation Toolkit*. She has done what most other authors on the subject of dreams have failed to do—empower people to interpret their own dreams. Instead of vague, ambiguous ideas on dream interpretation, Sylvia gives you all the tools you need to know how to understand the Holy Spirit's nighttime parables. Bravo on a great job of empowering believers to hear the heart of God, understand it, and share it."

—**Tom Scarrella**, *Scarrella Ministries, Ft. Lauderdale, FL*

"This is absolutely, without a doubt, one of the best dream interpretation books I have read. In *Dream Interpretation Toolkit*, Sylvia will teach you a solid biblical foundation for dream interpretation that she has learned through years of study. I highly recommend this book to anyone wanting to learn how to properly interpret their dreams, and to those who desire to grow in the prophetic."

—**Pastor Chris Mathis**, *The Summit, Crestview, FL*

"Thank you Sylvia, for aligning us with God's intentions for dreams. We spend about one-third of our lives sleeping and dwelling in the dimension of dreams. Sylvia helps us recapture this valuable time for the proper (not flaky) purposes for which God intended—to glorify Jesus, to heal, to restore, to set on track, and to help in a creative, mind-blowing variety of ways that only God can do. Reader, read on and enjoy an equipping book that is wise and scripturally solid."

—*M. John Cava*, *Director, World Outreach Center, Ft. Mill, SC*

"Everywhere we go, we meet people having dreams and asking, 'What does it mean?' Often dreams are left without interpretation or application, or worse, misinterpreted and causing harm to the dreamer or others.

Sylvia has written a masterful and practical book that will help both the young and mature believer receive what the Lord is revealing in their dreams. *Dream Interpretation Toolkit* helps us interpret and apply dreams with understanding and wisdom, and avoid the pitfalls common with dream interpretation.

Fifty years ago, I seriously studied dreams and their interpretation, including twelve years of university education. After I became born again, I set it all aside, working only infrequently with dreams for forty years—until now. Through *Dream Interpretation Toolkit*, the Lord has encouraged, instructed, equipped, and led me to move forward once again in working with dreams—to help others and myself experience greater intimacy with the Lord and become more Christ-like. May you and many others also be edified by these prophetic and practical understandings."

—*Lee LaCoss*, *Light of Life Ministries, Okanogan Valley, WA*

"Chris and I have known Sylvia for many years, and have seen the Lord take her through a huge learning curve that has been very hard at times. Yet she persisted, determined to understand this complex language. *Dream Interpretation Toolkit* is the result. She has done an exemplary job in her thorough, excellent Scriptural treatment of a topic that so many misunderstand.

For years, Chris has dreamed many vivid dreams, all of them filled with symbols. We were often discouraged—we knew the Lord was speaking, but we could not get His point. After reading this book, he had yet another dream. This time we followed her instructions and—there it was—the meaning was clear!

Thank you, Sylvia, for paying the price and laboring to bring us *Dream Interpretation Toolkit*. We heartily recommend it."

—**Chris and Hope Allen**, *Ft. Mill, SC*

DREAM

INTERPRETATION

TOOL KIT

Practical Tools to Interpret Your Dreams *tomorrow*

SYLVIA JACKSON

angel&company

DREAM INTERPRETATION TOOLKIT by Sylvia Jackson
www.dreaminterpretationtoolkit.com
Sylvia Jackson Ministries Inc.
Niceville, FL 32578

ISBN: 978-0-9905064-0-9
ISBN: 978-0-9905064-1-6 (e-book)
Printed in the United States of America

Published by Angel & Company LLC
P.O. Box 1376
Los Angeles, CA 90078
Cover Design by Kevin Lepp and Tiffany Taylor
Book Layout by Kevin Lepp

TABLE OF CONTENTS

ACKNOWLEDGEMENTS

Thank you, Lord, that even when I wanted to trade the gift of interpretation for something less complicated and controversial, You gave me the tenacity to keep digging for understanding and then taught me hidden mysteries.

Thank you, Brooke, for the years you heard my every dream, and we dug deep to understand dream interpretation. Thank you, Deborah, for being in tune with the Lord and encouraging me to finish this book. Thank you, Hope, for the endless hours you spent listening, encouraging, proofing, and believing in the Lord's call on me. Thank you, Jane and Candace, for reading the manuscript and helping edit and proof it early on.

Thanks to all of you who shared your dreams and stories that contributed to this book, and a big thanks to those who wrote endorsements.

Thank you, Kel, for believing in the gifting and seeing me grow in it through the years. I pray that you grow into the gifts and call of the Lord, and that you fulfill your destiny of the first man after God's heart in my family.

Thank you, Mother, for being my biggest fan. Thank you for the endless prayers you offered for Tif, for Kel, for all of your family, and for me. I'm so glad you saw the good fruit of some of it while you were here. For sure, you are in the great cloud of witnesses; I know you see this, and I know you're proud. Thank you for making this possible.

DEDICATION

Dearest Tif,

Without your help, I would not be as pleased with the outcome of *Dream Interpretation Toolkit* as I am.

Without your organizational skills, this book would have been nothing more than a stream of my consciousness put onto paper, from which few could decipher meaning, and fewer still, learn.

Without your intelligence, my writing would seem to be the works of an uneducated pen.

Without your prodding questions, I could never have discovered such amazing answers.

Without your great ideas, mine would be like ice cream without chocolate sauce or a wooden bowl.

Without your push toward excellence, I would have been finished months ago.

Love, Mom

FOREWORD

Having known Sylvia Jackson for the last several years, I am confident that you will be both blessed and challenged by her book. She is a very prophetic person and has always spoken clearly when giving a prophetic word to individuals or groups. She has written this how-to book in the same manner; in it she gives clear instruction to help a dreamer interpret their dreams. Anyone who is truly searching for answers to solve their own dreams will find help in this book.

During my sixty years in ministry, I've seen some people become "spooky spiritual" about dreams and I believe that's because of the lack of a good foundational understanding. This book will help us be aware of the importance of dreams and give us a Scriptural, practical, balanced way of putting them to work in our daily lives.

I am convinced that, as you read this book, dreams will come to mean more and have greater influence in your life with God. Even if you are only curious about dreams, it is a good read.

Dive in and enjoy the useful, helpful, healing contents of this book. You will be delighted you were able to gain insight and practical application, and you'll be able to put your dreams to work in your own life and in the lives of those dear to you. You will no longer be able to pass over your dreams lightly, but will experience fuller leading through them, along with continuing your consistent life of prayer and study of the Word of God, the Bible.

I recommend not only this book, but also my friend, Sylvia.

Dwight W. Edwards, DD
Pastor Emeritus of Champions Church, Winter Haven, FL

INTRODUCTION

Chances are good you're a dreamer since you've picked up this book. If you're new to dream interpretation and don't have a clue what dreams mean, but you're excited to receive vivid revelation from the Lord, I understand. I've been there. Years ago, I suddenly began having many dreams every night with no idea what they meant, but, like you, I was desperate to know. "Dream Interpretation Toolkit" will clarify that God does speak to us through dreams, teach you how to interpret and apply their messages, and show you that His love will lead you to healing and freedom.

Through years of searching Scripture and applying the principles found there, I learned many things, including a very big one—the Lord wants to heal us and uses *dreams* as one way to show us issues causing sickness. I've interpreted dreams for many people that brought healing in various areas—financial, mental, relational, physical, and spiritual.

Maybe you're not new to revelation or dream interpretation but you're frustrated or confused with trying to understand dreams. Perhaps you've been disappointed from things you thought would happen but didn't. I get it; I was too. For a few years I avidly read every dream interpretation book on the market and eagerly applied their principles, yet numerous times I was greatly disappointed by what I thought would happen and never did. Additionally, I made many mistakes trying to interpret my dreams and wound up disappointed and confused by the results. At times, doing something the wrong way is the best way to learn, and it seems the Lord lets us make mistakes, to teach us the right way so we can help eliminate those paths for others. This book will help you put any erroneous thinking about dream interpretation behind you, identify God's purposes in dreams according to Scriptural patterns, and acquire keys to understand correct interpretation.

Some pastors and church leaders have practically shut down conversations about dreams because they've been attacked by dreamers who claim that God "showed them the leadership's error" in dreams. Some of you have thrown out the baby with the bath water. Many dream interpretation experiences have been "flaky" and some in error, yet as leaders we want to know the Lord's reasons for giving dreams, apply Scripture, and learn a balance about revelation in order to see people healed and free.

There are some of you called to inner-healing ministry or counseling, and your clients tell you dreams that seem a bunch of gibberish. You don't know what they mean or how to help interpret, yet you know it's the Lord that's pouring them out. Putting the tools in this book to work for you will help you minister to people who are stuck and to navigate healing for others.

If any of this describes your experience with dream interpretation, you are the one for whom I've written this book.

In the last two decades, I've interpreted thousands of dreams for hundreds of people and taught dream interpretation seminars in various geographical areas. Scores of dreamers have learned to understand the Lord's messages in dreams, experienced a more intimate relationship with Him, and found healing for their body, mind, spirit, relationships, and finances. My hope is the same for you.

CHAPTER ONE

The Purpose of Dreams: to Lead Us to Jesus

Create in me a pure heart, O God, and renew a steadfast spirit within me —Psalms 51:10

It had been a hard year for James and Sandra. Due to the real estate crisis, his income as a part-time developer had all but disappeared and tithes from the small church they co-pastored had been hit hard.

The financial pressure had taken a toll on their nerves, and stabilization of the real estate market was nowhere in sight. James wanted to sell the family home, close his business, find a new pastor for the church, and move to Kenya, where he had ministered many times and had grown to love the people. He felt the Lord was working to close a door to their present location and to provide the money from the potential sale of their home in order to open a door to Kenya. *After all,* he reasoned, *the kids are grown now and don't really need us anymore.* Sandra wasn't at all keen on the idea and wanted to stay in

South Carolina to be around her three grandchildren. Additionally, the thought of selling the beautiful home she had painstakingly designed, and they had built during the real estate boom, was unthinkable. She wanted no part of spending the last chapters of her life in a third-world country. Arguing grew about God's will, along with constant strife.

During this time, Sandra had a dream in which she and James divorced and he married a young, pretty woman from Kenya. The dream bothered her tremendously at first, but as she thought about it for a few days, she began to consider the possibility that it might be best if they divorced and he married someone younger—someone from Kenya, the people he loved. After all, he had argued vehemently for some time that Sandra couldn't hear God. He always said she wasn't willing to let him be the head of the household; she wouldn't do what he believed was God's will—sell everything and move. She certainly was ready to end the fighting, and even let him go if that's what he wanted, but she would not sell her home and was unwilling to leave South Carolina. *Maybe this is God's will,* she thought. Perhaps He was telling her to put an end to the arguing and let the man do what was in his heart to do—minister full-time to those who desperately needed his spiritual gifts. Maybe she was in the way of his destiny, as James insisted. *But, after all these years,* she thought, *how could he leave so easily and break up the family? Doesn't he love me at all? Why God,* she thought in her heart, *would you want this? Do you really need a missionary that badly or am I just a terrible wife and horrible Christian?*

Finally, she told James about the dream, and he thought it could be confirmation of his desire to go to Kenya. As they pondered her dream, negative thoughts about their relationship continued to grow in them both. They decided to get a divorce so he could get on with his ministry and her with the family. They divorced and sold the house, and she moved in with one of the children. Soon after, she was diagnosed with an autoimmune disease.

The people in the fledgling little church struggled with their pastors' divorce and eventually disbanded. Some of the people took sides with James and some with Sandra.

James moved to Kenya, began a ministry, and met many young women who were excited with the potential to marry an American missionary.

This may seem like it was a dream from the enemy, but in fact it was from the Lord. However, the enemy certainly used it for his purposes. The divorce and church failure were caused by a misinterpreted, misapplied dream.

Had Sandra or James understood God's purpose for giving dreams and how to correctly interpret and apply them, the breakup of a marriage, family, and church might have been prevented, and, as we'll explore later in this book, Sandra possibly could have been saved from illness.

The root purpose of dreams is to purify our hearts and lead us closer to Jesus. Like all else, dreams and all other revelation exist for Jesus and the Cross. He came to do the ministry proclaimed in Isaiah 61, which he repeated in Luke 4: to save; to heal; to deliver from bondage; to bring favor; and to destroy the devil's works, which are to steal, kill and destroy, according to John 10:10.

At the root of many dreams is the Lord's motive to continue working those exact intentions: to save, heal, deliver, and give us direction to live the life for which He paid. His ministry toward us has not changed. He is anointed for these exact reasons; look for them as you solve your dreams and receive His ministry. Learning this aspect of dreams can bring a huge shift in your relationship with the Lord. He loves you.

God doesn't bring division or speak against His word in any way. Sandra's dream was incorrectly interpreted, and the misinterpretation seemed to indicate God's plan for their future. Even though events did transpire that caused the dream to "come true," it wasn't the Lord's intention for these things to happen.

Rather than foretelling the future, most dreams are symbolic and for healing or direction, which often comes from correction of our intentions. In Sandra's dream, the Lord was exposing her attitude about the continuing argument with James. She had become angry and offended with him that he would dare sell her home and move her away from her family. She had come to the decision that it was fine for him to go on the ministry field and never come back. For all she cared, he could just leave her with her home and family. Instead of a literal divorce, the divorce part of the dream was symbolic—she had "divorced" herself from him. James' "marrying a young Kenyan woman" in Sandra's dream was also symbolic. To Sandra, James seemed to have "fallen in love" with another "woman"—Kenya. His "marrying" this new woman and "divorcing" Sandra symbolized Sandra's feeling, and offense, that James had divorced himself from her needs and was only thinking of this "new woman"—his potential ministry to Kenya.

James, when hearing the dream, also allowed thoughts of literal divorce and marrying a younger woman from Kenya to confirm his desire to move there and minister.

Why, I can hear some of you say, *didn't God give James a dream too?* Perhaps He did but James didn't remember it, or maybe the symbols didn't readily seem to apply to the situation. *Then why didn't God just tell him?* No doubt He did, but James didn't hear His whisper or sense a tug at his heart, because he was entertaining thoughts of leaving. The Lord is always talking to us because He loves us and He came to save, heal, and deliver us. Acts 7:51 says that at times we are stiff-necked, don't hear God well, and resist the Holy Spirit. Like James and Sandra, when our mind is made up about a situation, we too can become stiff-necked and consequently go through difficult circumstances. God tries to make it easy for us in the beginning of a particular situation, but, if we ignore His voice or don't perceive it, He has no choice but to make it harder until we learn from our mistakes.

God Heals through Dreams

The result of the interpretation and application of Sandra's dream was bad fruit, negative results. In situations such as this, we could think the dream came from the enemy because God would never speak for us to divorce. In so thinking, we would miss God's point in the dream. As in Sandra's story, God often uses dreams not to foretell the future, but to expose our error so we will repent; get our hearts, minds, and attitudes right; and avoid consequences of our intended actions and reactions.

At times, the consequences from not only our intentions, but also our misinterpreted dreams, can be severe. Finding the true secrets hidden in dreams can prevent sickness and even death.

Scripture gives us patterns to help interpret dreams. One of the foundational patterns is found in the Bible in the 33rd chapter of Job. According to those Scriptures, some dreams symbolically show issues causing our sickness and are meant to bring healing.

Healing means we can become sound and healthy again; we can get back on track, and alleviate anguish or distress. Through correctly interpreted and properly applied dreams, the Lord brings direction; physical, mental, emotional, spiritual, relational, and financial healing; and deliverance from all manner of diseases, mental illnesses, wrong mindsets, addictions, and compulsions.

Some Reasons We Get Sick

One of the most simple, yet important, things to know is that God is good and the devil is bad. God isn't making us sick. Jesus died for our sicknesses and disease as well as for our salvation. He is standing at the door of our hearts, wanting to heal us.

Exodus 15:22-26 gives insight into some causes of disease, including not hearing the Lord's voice, not heeding it, and not doing what is right in His sight.

In this story, after crossing the Red Sea, Moses led the Israelites into the Wilderness of Shur, where a fountain of water was supposed to be located. However, they travelled for three days and found no water. Some of that enormous travelling crowd thought they were dying from thirst, and some had children that hadn't had a drink in three days. The group was grumpy, losing faith, angry, and bitter against Moses and God.

Finally, they came upon a fountain of water named *Marah*, meaning *bitterness*. The water there was undrinkable, and no doubt, the disappointment made their attitudes worse. When they complained, Moses prayed. God highlighted a tree to him and told him to throw it into the bitter waters, so they would become miraculously fresh and sweet.

At a time of great stress and trauma, Moses turned to God for help instead of allowing anger and bitterness to have a place in his heart. God responded with instructions that created a miracle, and He caused the very place of trial to become a place of sweetness.

Seeing Moses' response to go deeper in Him rather than allow bitterness or other negative heart issues to overtake him, God used the situation to reveal a secret key about stressful situations and their connection to sickness and disease.

He told the Israelites to give careful attention to His voice of instruction, to listen intently to His commandments and laws. In so doing, He would not allow them to have any of the diseases that the Egyptians had experienced. He said that He was their healer, inferring He was not their destroyer.

Still today, God's words and ways will keep us from disease, while bitterness, anger, and the like will open us to it. There is a destroyer, and he wants you to react incorrectly to stressful and traumatic situations that he might gain a hold on your body or mind.

Legal Right

The Lord often brings correction through dreams, not because He's mean, angry or wants to punish us, but because He sees the enemy's plans against us and wants to free us from those evil strategies and devices. He wants to deliver us from the devil, who frames us using God's laws to bring sickness.

The devil does this by being a legalist. He accuses us to the Father, to each other, and even to ourselves. He uses the law of God against us to gain a legal right; he actually frames us with it according to Psalm 94:20. When we break God's laws, it gives him the authority to steal, kill, and destroy.

Who hasn't broken God's laws? We all do every day. That's why we need a Savior, and one of the reasons He gives dreams.

God gave the earth to men, according to Psalms 115:16, and told him to guard and tend it in Genesis 2:15. When Adam obeyed the serpent and disobeyed God, he relinquished his legal right of authority to the deceiver, Satan, and God then pronounced a curse on mankind. In time, Jesus came as the "second Adam" and lived a perfect life, totally obedient even to death on the Cross. This broke the curse on all mankind; however, until Jesus returns to rule the earth the Church must enforce His victory.

When we are disobedient to any part of the law of God, we leave ourselves open for Satan to steal, kill, or otherwise destroy our lives. When we repent and apply faith and forgiveness to the exact place we have been wounded or sinned, and tell Satan to leave just as Jesus did, we enforce the victory won on the Cross.

When we repent of our sin or any other way we have broken God's laws, the devil can no longer hold us captive, make us sick, or worse. However, sometimes we must use force to get him out—including the spiritual tools of faith, perseverance, and patience.

All Sickness Isn't from Sin

I'm not saying that all sickness follows this pattern. There are times the enemy attacks when we are innocent: Jesus was tempted in the wilderness and suffered a brutal death, yet He was sinless. In another Scriptural account, Jesus said a certain man's blindness was not because of his or his parents' sin, but so the Father would be glorified. This book deals with healing through dreams, not all reasons for sickness, nor all ways to be healed.

God is full of grace and is able to deliver us from any circumstance at any time. His Word says He expects us to seek Him for the hidden things. Many times, we must find the exact sin and repent in order to get healing or deliverance.

Again, the real purpose of dreams is to lead us to Jesus for Him to save, heal, deliver, and give us direction. Through this book, we'll explore how God uses dreams today.

Key Points in This Chapter:

- The root purpose of dreams is to purify our hearts and lead us closer to Jesus.

- The Lord wants to deliver us from the enemy, who uses God's laws against us to bring sickness.

- All sickness isn't from sin, but some is. Dreams can reveal root issues causing sickness, so that we can repent and find healing.

CHAPTER TWO

The Importance of Correct Interpretation and Application

I grew up in a family of golfers. Dad graduated from PGA Players School and was a teaching pro. As a teenager, he lost four fingers on his right hand in an accident, but he overcame the loss, practiced diligently, hit hundreds of practice balls daily, and became a phenomenal golfer. Mom was a great player too, and their conversations at dinner revolved around golf and the lessons he had taught that day. They often talked about bad golf swings, grips, and stances, and about mediocre golfers who didn't take lessons. These golfers practiced endless hours, but to no good avail, because they were just ingraining their bad golf habits. Dad always said, unless they took lessons, they would never know what they were doing wrong, or how to do it right, and they would never excel at golf, regardless of how many practice balls they hit.

The same principle applies to dream interpretation. In order to know what the Lord is saying and benefit from His messages, we must first learn the right way, then practice those things or the wrong habits will become ingrained.

Correct interpretation and application comes with pursuit and repeated effort. Some have the idea that dream interpreters are "born, not made," but anyone can learn to interpret their dreams. As in all areas of life, there is a time of consecration and study required. Singers, artists, musicians, pastors, prophets, teachers, and others will tell you this is true. Many are born with an ability to sing, teach, or play an instrument, yet the ones who truly excel are often those who diligently apply themselves toward practice of their God-given talent. The same holds true for dream interpretation: the more you study and practice, the better you become.

To fully grasp God's purposes and messages in dreams, we need to understand how to interpret them correctly *and* how the Lord wants us to apply the revelation they bring.

Years ago, when suddenly the Lord began giving me many vivid dreams, I was excited to receive messages from Him. During that time, I told some friends about a vivid vision I had experienced while asleep. In the vision, the sky was dark although ablaze with the brightest imaginable stars. I was on a hilltop, watching the stars as they danced and continually changed the look of the sky. The experience was so awesome; it's indescribable. My friends were in awe as they listened. Then a mentor who was sitting close by posed a question that changed my life, "So what does it mean?"

I was perplexed. *What does it mean?* I thought. *Wow. I have no idea.* Until that moment, I was content to just have revelation from the Lord. That question drove me to another level: to find out more about dreams, visions, and interpretation.

Regardless of whether you're new to dream interpretation or experienced, if you have a desire to know what your dreams really mean, it's a solid indication you are called to interpretation. You can learn to interpret and apply the revelation from your dreams. My hope is that, after reading this book, you'll be able to do that tomorrow.

For those who feel they understand how dreams work, and are confident in interpreting them, but are reading this book to pick up a key or two, the concept of application could be a new notion. When I say application, I mean the answer to "What do I do with this?" The application of dreams is not widely taught or discussed in the Church as a whole today. The Church is still maturing in dream interpretation and at the relative beginning in understanding application of revelation of any kind.

There are those in church leadership who have seen members of their flock burned by improper dream interpretation, and some have been "spiritually abused" by it themselves. It can be a frustrating experience for a pastor to hear a long, rambling, symbolic dream and have no idea what it could mean. Some tell me they hear them often. It can be a time-consuming part of their job, and time wasting as well, when the leader doesn't understand interpretation, much less application.

Leadership's frustration is magnified when they themselves appear as a "bad" character in a parishioner's dream. I've heard many stories of church or ministry leaders who were approached by one of their members with such a dream, believing that God had revealed the leaders' error through the dream. This experience is all too common and can create disastrous results. The Lord does not gossip about people in dreams. People, including those in leadership, are symbolic for something going on in the dreamer's life. (We'll get more into this in Chapter Three.) God's people are perishing for lack of knowledge.

Most Dreams Are Meant for the Dreamer

One central point we'll unfold in this book is this: Most dreams are for the dreamer. Most often, it's a message about you, for you, regardless of who is in the dream. Assuming that dreams are meant for those who appear as characters in our dreams, interpreting dreams as something that will happen in the future, and thinking dreams are for our church or the Church as a whole are common interpretation mistakes that can be quite detrimental.

I'm not suggesting these are never the interpretation, but I have seen many people's lives negatively affected by assuming their dream was for someone else. When we make these and other mistakes about dream interpretation, we miss the message God is giving us about a specific issue, or worse, we can cause damage to others by incorrectly assuming our dreams are for them. We could be off the course of His path for our lives or we could be sick (physically, emotionally, spiritually, or financially) because we don't understand the true meaning of the dream.

Incorrect interpretation is a source of pain throughout the Church. Paul wrote to the Corinthians, "A little leaven leavens the whole lump." This is true about dream interpretation also. Incorrect interpretation can infiltrate our understanding of revelation and leaven the whole in a negative manner.

The Church is in a learning phase with dream interpretation. Though He has always given dreams, the gifts are being restored during their awakening over the last hundred or so years, and the magnitude of dreams being given in this time in history is unprecedented. As Peter said on the day of Pentecost in Acts 2:17-18:

> *And it shall come to pass in those days, says God, that I will pour of my Spirit on all flesh, and your sons and daughters shall prophesy and your young men shall see visions and your old men shall dream dreams (KJV).*

With this unprecedented "pouring" of dreams, the Church is struggling to understand His purposes for them and to learn to interpret them correctly. Learning dream interpretation is a relatively new study for the average believer.

Paul wrote to the Corinthians, *When I was a child, I spoke and thought and reasoned as a child.* Childish behavior and reasoning is expected for all children; it's natural and normal. When my daughter was barely two, her job was to empty the dishwasher. She was much shorter than the countertop, and would grab a clean plate with both hands, heave it above her head, and stack them up for me to put away. It was a slow, painstaking process but necessary for her to learn and participate in chores. As she grew, she was able to do the job entirely alone and much faster.

It's the same for us individually and for the Church as a whole. We are as children in the realms of dream interpretation and application. We are growing, learning, and finding God's true purposes and messages. We have made mistakes and will continue to make some as we learn, and that's okay. He has grace and patience for us, and let's have those attributes for ourselves, and for one another, while pressing for Truth.

Truth always leads us to Jesus. Proper interpretation will always lead us to Him and His healing, salvation, deliverance and direction. Dreams are one form of prophetic revelation, and the true spirit of prophecy reveals the purposes for which Jesus came.

There are three necessary elements required to receive a full understanding of dreams—revelation, interpretation and application. Revelation is supernatural communication from the Lord to mankind (the dream itself), interpretation explains the dream's meaning, and application shows us what we should do with the dream's interpretation.

Without proper interpretation, we have little more understanding than a "clanging cymbal," as Paul wrote in 1 Corinthians. A dream, however interesting, without a correct interpretation has little spiritual value.

Job 33:23 tells us dream interpreters are one in a thousand; however, this slender ratio isn't because the Lord set those numbers into stone like the Ten Commandments. There are so few because learning to interpret God's language isn't an easy task. Isaiah wrote, *He is a God who hides Himself.* Some very wise men in the book of Proverbs wrote that it's our glory to search out those things He conceals. He hides on purpose so we will seek.

Story of Revelation, Interpretation, and Application

I met Sheila at a church home group one night and afterward we were talking about her dreams over a cup of coffee. She had a story about revelation, interpretation, and application and how the three had worked together for her.

"I had been complaining to my sister about the amount of time I had waited on the Lord for His choice of a husband for me," she told me. "My sister laughs easily and I like to say funny things to make her laugh, so I jokingly said 'God is so slow, His middle name should be *Slow.*' I immediately felt convicted that I was speaking disrespectfully about the Lord, but sort of shrugged it off and made a mental note not to do that again.

A few nights later, the Lord spoke to me as I slept."

The Revelation

"I have a riddle for you. What is Pocahontas's middle name?" He said.

When Sheila said this, I suddenly sat straight up in my chair. This dream piqued my interest. "A riddle!" I interjected. "I've never heard a riddle from the Lord except the one in the Bible."

"Me either!" Sheila exclaimed. "So I thought, *How fun*! I jumped out of bed to do what I usually do when I hear Him speak something quizzical," she explained, "even though I had tried that kind of thing before without good results—I did a computer search for Pocahontas to find her middle name and didn't find it."

The Interpretation

"While online, I did see a sketch of Pocahontas standing between her husband-to-be, John Smith, and her father. John was kneeling on the ground, bound hands and feet, as her father held a hatchet to kill him. She stood between them with her hand up to stop her father. I realized she had put herself in the middle of a dispute between her father and the man she would eventually marry. In other words, she stood in the gap, doing the work of an intercessor for her husband.

Before this dream, I believed He would ultimately cause circumstances to line up for me to meet the one of whom He had spoken, but I hadn't actively, fervently prayed for it. After the dream, I thought I fully understood His point in the riddle, repented, and committed myself to pray."

The Application

Even though she received revelation and understood the correct interpretation, there was something missing, but she didn't yet realize it. It took a few days for the full application to hit her. "I thought I understood the Lord's entire intention in the riddle—to actively intercede rather than passively believe."

"I had a big 'Ah-ha' moment when I realized the rest of the story—the application. Driving down the road, not thinking about the dream at all, a whisper suddenly dropped into my thoughts, 'You say my middle name should be *Slow* but the problem is not Me. Your middle name should be *Intercessor*. You're not praying.'"

"This time I totally got it," Sheila said. "I repented for disrespect toward the Lord and for blaming Him for being slow, when the whole time the problem was me and my attitude toward the Lord."

The moment she called the Lord *Slow*, Sheila had felt a tug at her heart, conviction from the Holy Spirit. That was the reason He gave her the dream: the issue with her attitude, the issue of her heart.

At the same time, she learned a huge life lesson from this experience: the Lord expects us to pray in an active manner in order to bring change in our lives and in the earth, not just simply believe that He is sovereign and He will take care of it if that is His will.

Most applications will be an understanding to repent, forgive, change directions, and grow in the fruit of the Spirit.

It's not enough to receive revelation from the Lord in dreams and other spiritual experiences. It's important to learn to interpret them correctly, and to apply the interpretation to our lives in the way the Lord intended.

Key Points in This Chapter:

- In order to know what the Lord is saying through dreams and benefit from the messages, we first learn the right way, and then practice those things, or the wrong habits will become ingrained.

- There are three components of all revelation, including dreams—revelation, interpretation, and application. The correct understanding of each element is required in order to receive the full comprehension of a dream's meaning and purpose.

- A dream without correct interpretation has little spiritual value. It's important to learn to interpret dreams correctly, and to apply the interpretation to our lives in the way the Lord intended.

- Most dreams are for the dreamer.

- Truth always leads us to Jesus. Proper interpretation and application will always lead us to Him, and healing, salvation, deliverance and direction.

CHAPTER THREE

How to Interpret: Understanding Dream Patterns

When I was just two or three years old, I stayed with my grandmother while my parents worked. Granny was a skilled seamstress who sewed everything from draperies to wedding dresses. It was a normal day for her to take everything off the kitchen table, then cover it with a new piece of fabric, pin a pattern on top, and begin to cut.

She taught me how to make patterns for my doll's clothes, and I would sit at her feet and cut out the next lovely ensemble for my favorite dolly while she sewed on the old Singer machine.

Early in my sewing education, I saw the importance of patterns. I learned that if the pattern wasn't pinned onto the fabric correctly, the outcome would be haphazard. If you have ever sewn a garment from scratch, you know what a mess you can make if you don't follow the pattern.

There is a correlation between making garments using patterns and interpreting dreams. Dreams in Scripture tend to be in patterns, according to God's purpose in giving the dream. Once we see the patterns in Scriptural dreams, we can have a better idea if ours are meant for healing that comes through correction, or for instruction, warning, or foretelling.

The Lord is a creative Pattern Maker. I'm not suggesting that God always works everything in understandable patterns or that He is a calculable entity. However, He did put certain patterns into creation, including the way humans, animals and plants are made. We can count on these patterns. He can do anything, anytime He wants, and can speak outside the usual patterns, but that's not the normal way He does things. He is a God of order, not confusion. He is constant, as is His creation.

He also speaks in patterns throughout Scripture; one example is when He gave Moses specific patterns to build the Tabernacle.

Patterns, types, symbols, riddles, parables, and puzzles are part of the way God reveals Himself to us. As we study these, we learn keys that unlock hidden mysteries in the Bible and in other ways He speaks.

We can't solve the puzzles He gives us in dreams without knowing His language. He tells us plainly in Isaiah 55:8 that His thoughts and ways aren't the same as ours. They are higher and much different. We can't expect to understand how to solve His puzzles using our own language and understanding, but He's given us patterns in Scripture as a way we can learn how He speaks though dreams.

Things of the Spirit, whether prophecy, parables, dreams or other revelations, are rarely meant the way they appear at first glance. It takes study and prayer to dig deeper and find the treasures hidden beneath the surface.

The kind of pattern in which a dream is given shows its purpose. When we use patterns as a grid to understand how to interpret dreams, we find God's purposes in giving them become clearer. Once we know His purpose, we can then know whether the dream was given to correct us in some way (correction doesn't always mean we have done something displeasing to Him), to give direction, as a prophetic word for someone else, or to tell us of a future event. Once we know the reason behind a dream, it becomes easier to solve the puzzle it contains. Knowing His purpose is a very important key to finding the true meaning hiding inside a dream.

Dream Patterns in Scripture

There are numerous dreams in the Bible but only a few different patterns:

1. Job 33/Symbolic Dreams

2. Voice or Appearance of the Lord or an Angel

3. Foretelling Dreams/Dreams With Numbers

4. Dreams for Others

Pattern One: Job 33/Symbolic Dreams

The majority of dreams are highly symbolic, meant to bring healing, and are of the Job 33 category. These dreams reveal, through symbols, what we are doing or thinking that is contrary to Spiritual laws, or things that are against the Lord's plan for our lives. As we will see, incorrect thoughts/intentions or actions/reactions can cause sickness and lead to death. This pattern of dreams can bring conviction of our incorrect thoughts or intentions to prevent sickness from coming upon us, or it can move us to repent for what we've already incorrectly done or thought, in order to heal us.

At times, this pattern of dreams will show us direction through the correction they contain. The main point of this book is for us to learn to interpret the great majority of dreams according to the Job 33/ Symbolic pattern. We expound upon this pattern in Chapter Four.

Pattern Two: A Voice or Appearance of an Angel or the Lord

Another pattern of dreams is hearing the voice of an angel or the Lord as you sleep. In these, there is no mental picture, as in most dreams, or the only picture you see is that of the Lord or an angel. These dreams give the dreamer specific direction, warning, foretelling, or instruction. These tend to be clear and exact rather than symbolic.

Pattern Three: Foretelling Dreams/ Dreams with Numbers

Dreams with specific numbers are rare, but they can be foretelling. In Scripture, many of the dreams that were of a foretelling pattern had numbers in them.

Even foretelling dreams can have an element of implied correction, especially if they contain symbols. Similar to Job 33/Symbolic dreams, these dreams are meant to bring some kind of correction or instruction. Then a change must be made, whether in attitude, mindset, or direction, so the foretelling part can occur. If the dream is foretelling judgment, this pattern brings conviction so that any dire consequences can be prevented.

Pattern Four: Dreams for Others

Usually dreams are all about you. Although another person plays the star character or a minor role in your dream, that person is usually symbolic for a part of you. It is best to apply your dreams toward your own life.

Incidentally, you are never symbolic for another person or the Church in your own dream. When you dream of yourself, the dream is about you and for you.

When dreams are truly for another person, they often have implied correction or direction of some kind in the dream, but it comes in a mild form that is more like encouragement. For example, my mom used to serve up correction-encouragement sandwiches like, "Baby, I like your hair blonde and would like it even more if it was more blonde." Her correction was slight and implied, while at the same time giving me a compliment.

If you commit to try to interpret your dreams according to these patterns, you'll find the great majority of them fall into these categories. You will also find the most important thing the Lord wants to do through them: He wants to heal you and set you on the right path.

We will discuss dreams that are truly meant for others in Chapter Eight.

Key Points in This Chapter:

- Scriptural patterns show if our dreams are meant for healing of some area in our lives that comes through correction, or for instruction, warning, or foretelling.

- Dreams in Scripture tend to be in patterns according to God's purpose in giving the dream.

- The kind of pattern in which a dream is given shows its purpose.

- There are four different patterns of dreams in Scripture:

  1. Job 33/Symbolic dreams

  2. Voice or Appearance of the Lord or an Angel

  3. Foretelling Dreams/Dreams with Numbers

  4. Dreams for Others

CHAPTER FOUR

Understanding the Job 33/ Symbolic Pattern

Over 95% of dreams are filled with symbols and fall into the Job 33 category. We will cover the other patterns in later chapters so that we can differentiate between them; however, the main point of this book is for us to learn to interpret dreams of the Job 33/Symbolic pattern, and get the conviction, healing, and direction they bring.

All dreams of this Job 33/Symbolic pattern are filled with symbols, and understanding symbolic dreams can be a frustrating experience. These are the kind of dreams often described as "weird" and can be long and rambling, containing two or more scenes at times.

When you don't know the answer to a matter your best choice is not to allow frustration to win, but to dig in deeper with the Lord, ask and continue asking, believing He will answer until you have an answer from Him. Years ago, at a time of huge disappointment from the results of misinterpreted dreams, I sought Him for answers and experienced a season of revelation as He gave me keys of dream interpretation. In my sleep one night He said, "You have a Job 33 ministry." This proved to be the most important key I've learned about dreams and their connection with healing.

Job Chapter 33 reveals five steps that show how many dreams work.

Job was very sick, had lost his material goods, and all his children had died in an accident—he was totally miserable. He was in a terrible state, one that few people experience. His wife said, "Curse God and die," and three of his friends condemned him at length, though they had no true answers for his malady.

Job cried out to God, and it seemed He didn't answer. Job was struggling and growing bitter and angry, declaring that God "had it in for him" for no good reason.

Many people can identify with Job's situation. Life holds difficult, extremely hard circumstances for us at times. It can seem like those times when we need Him the most that He doesn't answer, and sometimes we get angry and blame Him for ignoring us. Sometimes people say they can hear God for anyone else but not for themselves. In these cases, there is often more happening spiritually than is readily apparent. If you can relate to this scenario and are mad with God, let's look at Job's situation and you'll find some answers, or at least purpose for the pain.

We often hear of Job's three friends, but there was a fourth man, Elihu, who had listened attentively to the conversation between Job and the others and disagreed with them all.

In the following passages, Elihu described the stages that take place as God speaks to us through our dreams about our heart issues. He describes a sequence that begins with 1) the Lord speaking to us about a troublesome situation but we don't hear Him; then 2) a dream is given, but if we don't understand its meaning; then 3) next we can experience a downward progression of sickness, more serious sickness, and even death.

Understanding that our heart issues cause this negative set of circumstances to occur gives us the opportunity to repent and be healed.

Job 33:14-29 unveils many hidden secrets about dreams, sickness, and healing.

> *For God does speak—now one way, now another —though man may not perceive it (Job 33:14 NIV).*

> *In a dream, in a vision of the night, when deep sleep falls upon men as they slumber in their beds, then he opens the ears of men, and seals their instruction, that He may withdraw man from his purpose, and hide pride from man. He keeps back his soul from the pit and his life from perishing by the sword.*

> *He is chastened also with pain upon his bed, and the most of his bones with strong pain: So that his life abhors bread, and his soul hates dainty meat. His flesh is consumed away, that it cannot be seen, and his bones that were not seen stick out. Yes, his soul draws near to the grave, and his life to the angel of death.*

> *If there is a messenger with him, an interpreter, one among a thousand, to show unto man his uprightness: then He is gracious to him and says, Deliver him from going down to the pit, I have found a ransom. His flesh shall be fresher than a child's; he shall return to the days of his youth: he shall pray unto God and He will be favorable to him; and he shall see his face with joy; for he will render unto man his righteousness. He looks upon men, and if any say, I have sinned, and perverted that which was right, and it didn't profit me...*

He will deliver him from going into the pit, and his life shall see the light. Look, all these things God works all the time with man... (KJV).

Elihu understood that God does speak about the issues of our heart (especially the issues that are separating us from Him) through dreams. He will speak to us directly about our intended incorrect actions or reactions to a particular situation but sometimes we don't realize it. He then gives us a symbolic dream, a puzzle of sorts, to bypass our normal way of thinking. If we don't react to the initial conviction from the Holy Spirit about the issue and then fail to understand the conviction that comes in the dream, the enemy can use our intentions and mindset against us and we could get sick. If we continue in our wrong mindset about the situation that occurred, we can get sicker and sicker and even die. This progression is evident as you read Job's story. There is a remedy for this: correct interpretation and repentance.

The above scriptures are quoted from the 33rd chapter of Job, however look back to the 7th chapter. At this earlier point, he was complaining about having terrifying dreams.

When I say, My bed shall comfort me, my couch shall ease my complaint, then You scare me with dreams, and terrify me through visions; so that my soul chooses strangling, and death rather than my life. I loathe it; I would not live always: let me alone; for my days are vanity (Job 7: 13-16 KJV).

Job had terrible dreams, and they were so bad he wanted to die rather than continue living. Notice he credited the terrifying dreams to God, not the enemy, and asked Him to leave him alone, not give him any more dreams or visions, and just let him die.

Job accused Him of doing nothing to help and blamed Him for the losses, destruction, sickness, and torment because he didn't know God's ways about dreams. Job had no idea God had been trying to tell him for some time, through dreams, about the strategies of the enemy against him.

Many of us have this experience—the worse the circumstances become, the worse our dreams are. Sometimes we get mad with God and want peace and rest, often during difficult times, and instead get horrible, graphic dreams. He wants us to interpret the dreams to see what He's revealing about our emotional reactions and more. Meanwhile we want to run away from Him, the circumstances, and the dreams. He's talking and we're rejecting His language, yet blaming Him for not talking because we don't understand this way He communicates.

Job said his dreams were terrifying. (The ones that show the enemy working in our lives usually are scary, and so are some that are given to correct our intentions.) These dreams are always symbolic ones, not literal or foretelling. Symbolic dreams are always speaking to us about issues of our hearts.

Jesus said the enemy came to kill, steal, and destroy and his tactics haven't changed. Whenever we succumb to negative or ungodly thoughts, we have come into agreement with him, and Job's agreement was obvious—he said he wanted to die.

Let's look at the progressive steps in this kind of dream, as outlined by Elihu in Job 33, in more detail.

Step One—God Does Speak

> *For God does speak—now one way, now another—though man may not perceive it (Job 33:14 NIV).*

He does speak. The Bible is a story of God's communication with mankind. Jesus said in John 10:27, "*My sheep hear my voice, and I know them, and they follow me.*"

The most common topic He addresses in dreams is our heart issues, those things that are troubling us, or that are against His laws or will for our lives. At this first stage, He tugs at our hearts saying, "Don't do this, don't think this way, let it go, etc." Sometimes people address this stage as "a check in my spirit," or a feeling of conviction. He will speak to us about anything that causes concern; however, it's not easy to hear Him or perceive conviction when our emotions are high. One reason we don't always hear Him is because we have chosen to do things our own way in a particular situation, and consequently our hearts, thoughts, and opinions become calloused in that area.

Sometimes it seems the Lord doesn't speak to us while we are trying to handle a troublesome situation, but these verses say He does, we just don't always perceive Him speaking. Even though we don't always hear Him, He loves us and keeps trying to communicate. Our emotions can speak louder than His whispers, but He doesn't leave us without hope or direction. He gives us dreams to bring more conviction, and He continues to stand at the door of our hearts and knock.

Step Two—He Gives Us a Dream

If we miss His first attempt to get our attention, He tries it a different way—we often are given a dream.

> *In a dream, in a vision of the night, when deep sleep falls upon men as they slumber in their beds, then he opens the ears of men, and seals their instruction. (Job 33:15-16)*

The word instruction in the above verse, according to Strong's Concordance, is the Hebrew word *musar,* which is more correctly translated as *chastening, discipline, or correction.* The word *ozen,* interpreted in the above Scripture as *ears,* is a figurative word meaning *receiving revelation.*

An easier way to understand this verse is to think of it this way: when we're sleeping, the Lord opens our "revelation receiver," puts in a symbolic dream, then seals us back up with the chastening, correction, or discipline inside.

Elihu, then, was explaining to Job that the Lord did speak about his issues, but Job didn't perceive it, so he had a dream with correction of some kind hiding in it, because He corrects those He loves.

Take the Sting out of Correction

Don't allow negative feelings about the word *correction* cause you to build a wall against it. Correction doesn't always mean you have done something wrong or sinned. It doesn't necessarily mean the Lord is pointing out your mistakes or judging you as bad. Correction can also mean the Lord is attempting to adjust your thinking, to help you better handle life's difficulties, get you going in the right direction, or put you in His best plan for your life. He corrects us to help save us from the enemy's evil plans.

A dream with symbols can also indicate that something is not yet clear or that the Lord will give you more information later. Both of these situations also mean He is correcting our path.

Most Symbolic Dreams Are about Recent Events

Job 33/Symbolic dreams are given to correct our path, which often means our attitude, point-of-view, or emotional response to a troublesome situation we encountered *that day or perhaps the day before.* Understanding this key is another important element for correct interpretation.

If you view the majority of your dreams as a course correction about events that occurred a day or two before you had the dream, rather than something you expect to happen in the future, you will have a huge shift in understanding, interpretation, and application. You will begin to understand the way He speaks in dreams about what's on your heart and mind; you'll draw closer to Him and your heart will be clearer.

Most symbolic dreams aren't for tomorrow or the future; they are about our heart and what we dealt with either yesterday, the day or two before, and, on occasion, in our distant past.

If you grew up in an environment that causes you to believe God is angry with you and meting out punishment whenever you think of the word *correction*, be assured that's not His intention. He loves you so much He gave His Son to literally die for you because He doesn't want to punish you.

Giving the devil his dues: He has done quite a job convincing people that God is mean and out to get you, when in fact, it's the devil who is the mean one. He's out to steal from you, kill you, and destroy your life. God wants to rescue you from the enemy's plans against you. That's why He brings needed correction. Like a good Daddy, He sees more than the child sees, and is teaching, leading, correcting, instructing; He's not beating up His kids.

The Lord doesn't bring correction to tear us down but as a necessary tool to build us up. If we are headed the wrong way and not corrected, we won't arrive at our destination. We could end up sick or, according to these verses in Job 33, we could even die prematurely if we aren't corrected. Remember, the devil wants to kill you. The Lord loves you and wants to heal, deliver, and set you on the path toward a good future and hope.

Often we think the wrong things or have a bad attitude. At times, we are fearful, wounded, or determined to have our own way. Regardless of our weaknesses, He loves us too much to leave us there. It's a sign of His love when He corrects and disciplines us.

> *"...for the Lord disciplines those He loves..."* *(Proverbs 3:12 NIV).*

> *"The fear of the Lord is the beginning of wisdom, but fools despise wisdom and correction..." (Proverbs 1:7 NIV).*

The Spirit knows our heart, intentions, and motives, and He wants to help us get them clean and keep them clean. We literally cannot know our own heart; almost everyone does what they think is right, but we are often unable to see clearly. Proverbs states it this way:

> *There is a path before each person that seems right, but it ends in death (Proverbs 14:12 NLT).*

Our hearts are calloused in areas. We often deal with strong mindsets and self-preservation that affect our intentions and motives.

> *The heart is deceitful above all things and desperately wicked, who can know it? (Jeremiah 17:9 KJV).*

The Lord corrects us through dreams to help us get our hearts right so we can be free, healthy and live in the fruits of the Spirit.

Prophecy is Public, Dreams are Private

Scripture tells us that prophecy is for *"edification, exhortation, and comfort"* (1 Corinthians 14:3). Bill Hamon of Christian International Ministries has an easy way to understand the reasons the Bible gives for personal prophecy: for building up, stirring up, and cheering up.

A point to consider about differences between prophecy and dreams—prophecy is said publicly, although publicly can be one-on-one. On the other hand, a dream is between you and the Lord, and unless you tell it, no one else knows. They are private, just like correction from your parents. Parents normally correct their children at home, not in public. That's how the Lord does it too; He commends you in front of others for your excellence and usually corrects your mistakes in private, like a loving Father.

Correction Saved My Life

Years ago, I had an experience that shows how valuable the Lord's correction can be. I truly believe His correction saved my life.

I was in a business deal with a person who cost me a good deal of money. I was upset when I found out about it, called Mom and talked for hours, telling her every detail. During the conversation, I had a nagging feeling to hang up the phone, quit talking about it. I kept talking. When we did hang up, I called my daughter and started the tirade again. The same Voice again whispered for me to stop talking about it. Finally, mentally and emotionally exhausted, I went to bed.

I awoke a few hours later by the sound of swords clashing in my kitchen. Terrified, I sat straight up in bed and saw angels and demons fighting over my life. Instantly I cried, "Lord, what did I do to allow this in my home?"

Just as quickly He spoke, "You refused to forgive. You did not obey Me and hang up the phone. You went to bed angry."

"Oh, Lord, please forgive me!" I loudly cried. Instantly they all disappeared. I was so scared I thought I would never sleep again. I got out of bed, turned on every light in the house, looked up Scriptures on forgiveness, then stayed up all night and forgave everyone I could think of for everything that had ever happened to me. Literally, the Lord spared my life that night by sending angels to fight for me.

Now that I understand how dreams work, I understand more of the application of what I saw in the Spirit that night. The enemy had come to kill me (that is what he does—steals, kills, and destroys). He had the legal right because of my disobedience, unforgiveness, and the anger I took to bed, but he lost the right and the battle the moment I repented.

Rebellion [disobedience] is as the sin of witchcraft... (1 Samuel 15:23 KJV). You shall not suffer [allow] a witch to live... (Exodus 22:18 KJV).

If you do not forgive others their sins, your Father will not forgive your sins... (Mark 11:26 NIV).

Do not let the sun go down while you are still angry... (Ephesians 4:26 NIV).

This scenario could seem dramatic to you. The idea that my life was in danger because of the sins that some of us deal with daily might seem far-fetched. I can't explain this further except to say the above verses are clear: we must forgive others, we must obey the Lord, and we must work through issues in our hearts before the day's end.

The Lord's angels fight for us in similar situations all the time but we are oblivious of it. The Lord opened my spiritual eyes in that situation so you and I would be aware that our actions have consequences, even dire ones, and that He is always working behind the scenes for our benefit.

Some people say angels are bored waiting on us to pray so they will have assignments, but perhaps they are extremely busy fighting for us in our ignorance and sin.

Step Three—Bypassing Strong Mindsets by Using Symbols

Elihu explained why God gives dreams in symbols: to keep us from doing what we have purposed to do.

> *[He gives dreams] that He may withdraw man from his purpose, and hide pride from man. He keeps back his soul from the pit and his life from perishing by the sword (Job 33:17-18 KJV).*

To recap the process to this point: we have a troubling event, He speaks to convict us from wrong actions or thoughts about the situation, but if we don't perceive His voice, He gives us a dream.

Most dreams are in symbolic form, because symbols bypass the strong mindsets that keep us from clearly seeing our own heart's intentions.

Many of our dreams are given to pull us away from what the above Scripture calls our purpose—what we intend to do, to think, or to feel. Jesus spoke in parables, which, like dreams, are meant to bypass our mindsets and intentions. Symbolism is used the same way in dreams.

When asked why he spoke in parables Jesus said:

...this people's heart has become calloused; they hardly hear with their ears, and they have closed their eyes. Otherwise they might see with their eyes, hear with their ears, understand with their hearts and turn, and I would heal them (Matthew 13:15 NIV).

Parables aren't easy to understand, and neither are many dreams. He explained that the hearts of the people were hardened, and this was why they could not "see or hear." In other words, they could not receive or understand the revelation He was speaking.

Most dreams are parables; parables are designed to cause us to introspect and seek Him for understanding. When we seek a dream's interpretation and proper application, He will expose our motives so we can see the truth about what we are doing, thinking, or feeling. Once we see the truth, we can repent, and then correct our hearts and/or course of action.

Daily, we act, react, think, or set our hearts to do or not do many things. We have dozens of opportunities to obey or disobey the leading of the Spirit. As Paul said, our spirits are willing but our flesh is weak. None of us lives a perfect, sinless life even for a day, probably not for an hour. Our motives are constantly self-centered and we are all in a sanctification process our entire lives.

While we are still in this earthly, life-long process, our hearts are calloused in areas and we can hardly hear His voice or see Truth in those places. He wants us to take the time to interpret the symbols in our dreams and search our hearts to find where we are calloused and determined to go our own way.

Step Four—Sickness and Death

If the Lord has spoken to us and then given us dreams, but we still don't understand that we are in need of some kind of adjustment, then at times we get sick.

He is chastened also with pain upon his bed, and the most of his bones with strong pain: So that his life abhors bread, and his soul hates dainty meat. His flesh is consumed away, that it cannot be seen, and his bones that were not seen stick out. Yes, his soul draws near to the grave, and his life to the angel of death (Job 33:19-22 KJV).

As believers we question, "Why are we sick? What's going on spiritually? Why are we not walking in divine health?" Sometimes the reason is that we aren't aware of our attitudes that have given the enemy legal right to our lives.

If we have failed to perceive our spiritual condition, we sometimes get sick, lose our appetite, and become sicker and sicker, until death is at our door.

Of course, sickness doesn't always follow this progression, but the Bible tells us sin and sickness can be directly correlated. For example, the Lord told the Israelites that if they obeyed Him, He wouldn't allow them to suffer the diseases of the Egyptians. In addition, Scripture indicates that sin causes some sicknesses, and these can be healed through repentance:

Confess your faults one to another and pray for one another that you may be healed (James 5:16 KJV).

There is more than one answer to the question, "Why do we get sick?" There are also many ways that God heals. Not all sickness is caused from issues in our hearts; however, some is. We want to hear God and repent every time our sickness is sin-related that we might live in health.

Step Five—Interpretation, Intervention

At this point, God sends someone to help. He sends an interpreter, an intercessor, a prophet, or counselor, even an angel, to help us understand where we went wrong.

> *If there is a messenger with him, an interpreter, one among a thousand, to show unto man his uprightness: then He is gracious to him and says, Deliver him from going down to the pit, I have found a ransom (Job 33:23-24 KJV).*

It's a good idea to know others anointed to minister in different spiritual areas and seek them out when issues arise that we can't seem to overcome; that's the idea of "body ministry." If we ask—although sometimes we must continue asking for a time—the Lord will send help. The one He sends will help the dreamer understand what they have done wrong, and help them find the way back. When we see our wrong and repent, God's favor begins to show in our life again, the downward spiral stops, and the Lord is able to redeem us from the enemy's strategy.

After God spoke to Job at great length, he realized he had been accusing God of wrongdoing and repented. This is what's called an "Ah-ha" moment. When we have a dream and realize the correct interpretation and application, we know it in our hearts.

Step Six—Health is Restored After Correct Interpretation

Once a dream is interpreted correctly, and the dreamer understands the meaning and prays accordingly, his life and health are restored.

> *His flesh shall be fresher than a child's; he shall return to the days of his youth: he shall pray unto God and He will be favorable to him; and he shall see his face with joy; for he will render unto man his righteousness. He looks upon men, and if any say, I have sinned, and perverted that which was right, and it didn't profit me...*
>
> *He will deliver him from going into the pit, and his life shall see the light. Look, all these things God works all the time with man... (Job 33:25-29 KJV).*

In other words, if a person realizes they have sinned then confesses and turns away from it, God will return them to right standing. This Scripture also says the Lord does this through dreams all the time.

Matthew 18:16 states that a matter is established when confirmed by two or three witnesses. Proverbs 8:33-36 verifies the information in Job 33, and draws a strong correlation between heeding correction to avoid sickness and death. Interpreting and paraphrasing these verses in Proverbs using the Hebrew Lexicon, they could read:

> *Heed discipline, correction, and chastening, deal wisely and don't refuse these things. Happy is the man who hears and watches daily for that correction, protecting himself and those he loves. For he who finds correction, discipline and chastening finds favor and life from Yahweh. But he who misses the correction injures his own body and mental state. All who reject correction are flirting with death.*

An Example of Healing through a Job 33/Symbolic Dream

Vickie and I met at a church service, and our common passionate interest in dreams provided a foundation for friendship. She and her husband Phil were raising their eight-year-old granddaughter, Sallie. One week after her birthday, Sallie suddenly came down with a serious blood disease. The doctors said there was no cure and sent the little girl home.

Over the next couple of weeks, her blood count rose slightly—but then started to fall. There was nothing else they could do, the doctors said.

Sallie couldn't attend school or play with friends. Over the next weeks, her blood count fell to a very low, scary number and continued a downward plunge. Vickie and Phil were praying and believing God for healing, yet there was no positive change.

Like her grandmother Vickie, Sallie was a dreamer, and a spiritual warrior. Though barely eight-years-old, she was a highly anointed singer, practically a child prodigy, and was in love with Jesus. No doubt, the enemy had a strategy planned against her at his first opportunity.

One day, as Vickie and I were on the phone, Sallie interrupted to tell me her dream from the night before. This particular dream showed an issue had occurred on her birthday and I began to ask questions.

Vickie explained that every birthday she baked a huge chocolate cake with chocolate icing for Sallie; it was the child's favorite part of her birthday. This year, Vickie had been sick with a stomach virus for a week before Sallie's birthday and couldn't physically handle the baking. She had promised Sallie earlier in the week that she would bake it, but she had no idea the sickness was going to be so persistent. Instead, on the special day, Vickie sent Phil to the grocery to buy a chocolate cake with chocolate icing, but the grocery had none so he bought a carrot cake.

Sallie was heartbroken, but she dared not say anything. Instead, she pretended to like the cake and stuffed down her offense. In her little heart, she didn't get the one thing she wanted the most—her grandmother's chocolate cake. The offense went into her heart and she was extremely angry with both grandparents but didn't tell them. She just kept it all in her heart, and as these things can do, it grew.

When I realized the situation the dream was addressing, I told them she should repent and forgive her grandparents. They, in turn, agreed to repent for provoking her to anger by not being faithful to their promises.

About six months had elapsed since Sallie's birthday and the onset of her sickness, but within two weeks of repenting and declaring the Scriptures, her blood count started to rise. After another few weeks, it was practically in a normal range. The doctors had no medical explanation for her healing and she returned to school. The only explanation was the Lord had shown the issue in a dream, there was repentance, and within weeks, she was healed.

Close Timeline between Trauma and Disease

There were seven days between her birthday, when Sallie was offended, and the day the disease was diagnosed. There can be a close timeline between the onset of anger, trauma, unforgiveness, offense, emotional wounding, stress, fear, resentment, or other negative actions or reactions, and the beginning of sickness. Most often, sickness begins within a few days of the issue, yet I have seen it begin within minutes.

Consider the trauma Jesus experienced in the Garden of Gethsemane and his body's immediate reaction. His agony was so great he sweated huge drops of blood, according to Luke 22:44.

Paraphrasing information found at www.wisegeek.com, the physical condition Jesus suffered is Hematidrosis, and is a condition where one's sweat contains blood. When one suffers extreme anguish—such as when facing their own death—tiny blood vessels first constrict, then dilate and rupture. Next, the blood effuses into nearby sweat glands.

Dealing with such trauma and sorrow—emotions mankind was never intended to handle—had begun its immediate curse on His physical body. He had already begun to die; He said so Himself:

My soul is overwhelmed with sorrow to the point of death (Matthew 26:38 NIV).

He didn't sin, wasn't angry or offended, but was greatly traumatized in His soul—His mind, will, and emotions—as He wrestled in the garden. At this point, He was facing suffering and death, and had begun to take all the sin and curse of the world upon Himself. He resisted all wrong thoughts, actions, and reactions to the point of sweating blood (Hebrews 12:4 KJV).

The timeline between the Lord's anguish and disease was immediate, and often ours is too.

Modern scientific thought agrees there is a link between anger, offense, trauma, and the possibility of immediate negative bodily reaction. The European Society of Cardiology substantiates this close timeline. Quoting that group, www.sciencedaily.com writes, "Outbursts of anger may trigger heart attacks, strokes, and other cardiovascular problems in the two hours immediately afterwards, according to the first study to systematically evaluate previous research into the link between extreme emotion and all cardiovascular outcomes."

Because there is a close timeline between the troublesome situation and the body's reaction, dreams that deal with the circumstances also come quickly, usually the same night or within a day or two.

Brenda, a widow for three years with two young daughters, met Steve, a very successful businessman who had come to her church as a speaker at a Christian business conference, and they connected immediately. Not one to be easily fooled, Brenda checked him out and found that his ex-wife, according to his friends' and family's stories, was "crazy" and mean, and had committed adultery while they were married. The picture was soon painted in Brenda's mind that the issues in his marriage were those of his ex-wife.

Steve was loving, kind, and sweet to her and her children, and Brenda fell in love with him quickly. Their kids connected easily, and all circumstances seemed to be lining up that this was the Lord's will for her future. She sold her home in California, left a great job with excellent benefits, married him, and moved to New Orleans where his business was located.

Within a few months, his roving eye began to surface and he seemed unable to control it. Although he was sweet and loving toward her, his now-obvious issues with lust became a constant struggle between them. After being married only six months, she received a call telling her he was seen walking into a hotel in the French Quarter with another woman.

Brenda was shocked. She had sold her home and left a great job, and only months later, her life and those of her children were in shambles—because of the actions of a "godly" man! She went to his office, confronted him, and her temper erupted violently.

They argued loudly. Then it got worse—he said she wasn't sensuous or beautiful enough to please him. Adding insult to injury, and refusing all personal responsibility, he blamed her for his affair, insulted her looks, and rejected her as a woman.

In a rage, she picked up their wedding picture from his desk and threw it into the trashcan, shattering the glass. She stormed out of his office, got into her car and screeched out of the parking lot. She was uncontrollably angry; she knew she had never been this angry before. She drove to their home, screaming and crying.

Within minutes, her head began to hurt, and the pain was like nothing she had ever experienced. When she opened her eyes, the sight of the room became frozen in her mind, like a camera that had taken a picture. She was violently nauseated from the pain and couldn't speak, move, or open her eyes without throwing up. She began hearing a very loud sound, like a whoosh, whoosh and realized it wasn't a strong wind outdoors, but the sound of her own blood pressure in her brain.

In her uncontrolled rage, her blood pressure had shot up to an alarming rate. Brenda knew instantly that she had allowed this, in fact even caused it, by her violent reaction to her husband's infidelity. She decided she had no choice but to forgive him, but it was going to be a hard task. She went to the doctor, who diagnosed her with severe migraines, and she started taking prescription drugs. For weeks after the occurrence, a migraine would trigger from any slight stimulus, and she had to take the medication and sleep for hours to stop the pain. Her violent reaction had altered her life in a significant way.

Brenda made a firm decision she would never lose her temper again. She repented and forgave her husband, and the migraines stopped entirely within a few months.

Brenda's very difficult, painful situation, but wrong choice of actions to it, triggered severe migraines that began within minutes of the situation. She suffered extreme sickness due to her intense anger, but she learned to make the right choices in such circumstances—to forgive, *to be angry and not sin. (Ephesians 4:26).*

Dreams of Your Past

There are seasons when the Lord gives dreams to clean up your past, and they will be of the Job 33/Symbolic pattern. These dreams often occur at a time of other inner-healing ministry or a new or renewed heart change by the dreamer. At times, circumstances will trigger unhealed areas in our lives and we will have dreams about those issues. These dreams will focus on one's past experiences, sometimes many years in the past rather than a day or two before the dream, and will point to a need for deliverance, forgiveness, or other healing.

Certain symbols are telltale signs that your dreams could be addressing past issues: your grandmother's home, a back door, back windows, or the back yard. Other symbols that can have a similar meaning are those in which things are stored away and forgotten, such as the garage, kitchen cabinets, a deep freezer, and a storage unit.

A class reunion or a family reunion usually indicates that your current actions or reactions are the way you handled situations in the past, and that you are doing things the same way again—you are "re-uniting" yourself with your past attitudes, thoughts, or actions.

These dreams occur when similar situations arise as those in the past, and you continue to handle them the way you did then. In other words, the situations and your actions/reactions about them are reoccurring, and so are your dreams about them.

Regardless of the time in one's life with which their dreams are dealing—whether current or past—the great majority of dreams are of this Job 33/Symbolic pattern. They are for the purpose of correction or instruction to bring God's love and healing to the dreamer.

Key Points in This Chapter:

- Job 33:14 –29 reveals six steps God uses to speak to us in many dreams, in order to save us from the enemy's strategies:

    1. He speaks to convict, correct, or instruct us in a particular situation but we don't perceive His voice.

    2. He gives us a dream that continues to convict, correct, or instruct us.

    3. He bypasses our mindset, intentions, or pride by giving the dream in symbols.

    4. If we don't understand the correct interpretation of the dream and/or don't make the necessary corrections, sometimes we get sick.

    5. He sends someone to help interpret the dream, bring wisdom or counsel. We have the opportunity to see the error of our ways and repent.

    6. If we repent, we are healed, set free, and become closer to the Lord.

- Many dreams are meant for God's kind correction.

- View your dreams as a course correction caused by events that occurred mostly either a day or two before you had the dream.

- He loves us and wants to heal, deliver, and set us on the path toward hope and a good future.

- Symbolism is often used to expose the intentions of our hearts, much in the same way Jesus spoke in parables.

- Sometimes we get sick because we aren't aware of our attitudes, places where we have ignorantly given the enemy legal rights.

- There is a close timeline between the troublesome circumstances that caused the dream and the sickness.

CHAPTER FIVE

Understanding the Symbols in Your Dreams

Now that we see most of our dreams are symbolic and for healing of some kind, let's look at some technical aspects of understanding symbolism.

Symbols are a type of figurative language used in Scripture and most other ways in which God speaks. This kind of language speaks to the heart more than our logical mind.

Symbolism is used to give a meaning to a word or phrase other than the obvious, expected meaning. A few common dream examples are:

- Using your home to represent your heart or your life

- Using an attorney to represent legalism

- Using a roller coaster to represent an emotional upheaval

The last chapter of this book provides a condensed dictionary of many common dream symbols. Look through it and you will have a better idea of what is meant by a symbol and how figurative language works. You will find it a good resource to identify meanings for the symbols in your dreams.

However, you will have symbols in your dreams that aren't included in the Symbol Dictionary and will need to know how to find the meanings. First, let's look at some foundational understandings of biblical interpretation, including the Principle of First Mention. We will then discuss other steps that will help you determine the meaning of symbols that show up in your dreams.

Principle of First Mention

The study of guidelines to interpret Scripture, called Hermeneutics, supports a Principle of First Mention, which means the first time a subject is mentioned in Scripture a fundamental pattern of its symbolic meaning is established. In other words, when we understand the use of the term in its first appearance, we can then apply that same meaning to other portions of Scripture and other ways God speaks, including dreams. He doesn't speak different languages in different methods of communication. His language is the same in dreams, visions, prophecy, and Scripture, although Scripture carries far more weight and certainty.

Sometimes the first time a word is mentioned in Scripture, its use is ambiguous. For example, the first time some colors are mentioned is in reference to the intricate details of the tabernacle's construction. In such cases, it's difficult to know the root meaning of that symbol, so we must go to the next time the term is mentioned, or perhaps the one after that.

The root meaning of a term found in its first mention will prove to have a similar meaning every time He uses it. Think of it like a tree. A tree has roots, a trunk, branches, and leaves. The primary meaning will be the root and similar meanings are like other parts of the tree.

For example, let's look at the color *red*. It's first mentioned in Genesis 2:19 as the name *Adam*, which is Hebrew for *red*, or *ruddy*. Another meaning for *Adam* is *blood-colored;* the Hebrew word *dam* is the word for *blood*. The first time man was called Adam was when he was given the task of naming all animals, each of which had blood as their life. Considering these first uses of red in Scripture, we find the root meaning of *red* is *blood*.

A branch meaning of *red* could be *love*, because we use a red heart to symbolize it, and the heart is the main vessel for blood. Another branch meaning is *life*, because ...*the life of a creature is in the blood (Leviticus 17:11 NIV)*. *Red clothing* most often symbolizes Jesus because His blood was shed on the Cross, and the book of Revelation says His garments were stained red. *Dark red* is the color of dried blood, and it symbolizes our hearts that once were wholly for the Lord yet now His blood is "old" or 'dried up" to us.

Aside from a root or branch meaning, symbols often are used for their slang meaning. For example, *red clothing* can also mean anger. Surprisingly, the Lord speaks in dreams using slang quite often. A person is said to be hot-blooded when they have anger issues. Sometimes a person will show up dressed in red clothing in a dream, be driving a red car, or have red hair when anger issues are addressed.

How to Find Meanings for Symbols

Again, the Symbol Dictionary in this book is a great first place to start. I compiled these meanings using the Principle of First Mention and the approaches below. When you have symbols that are not in this book, here are some helpful tips to help you find their correct meanings.

- Bible concordance: Many Bibles have a good concordance in the back that will lead you to verses in the order in which those words are used. That makes it easy to find the first use of the word.

- Look up the verses, meditate on the word's possible meaning according to how it's used in Scripture, pray, and ask the Lord to help you understand the meaning. As you read the references and explanations in the Numbers and Colors sections in the Symbol Dictionary, you will see how He uses figurative language in dreams.

- However, bear in mind a Bible concordance doesn't include all listings of a word, and its first uses could be missing. An exhaustive concordance is a better source, such as Strong's Concordance.

- Strong's Concordance: This comprehensive book lists every word, each time it's used, in the King James Version of Scripture. If you're doing an intense study on a symbolic term, this is a great resource.

- Dictionary: There are many free online dictionaries. Sometimes just looking up the dictionary meaning of the word and meditating on its possible symbolic meaning will give you clarity about its application in your dream.

- Computer search engines: At times, you must do more research on a term used in a dream because it doesn't appear in a dictionary or concordance. The Lord knows every word in every language, and at times will even speak in a language you don't know in a dream. A search engine will help you find foreign words as well as other terms unknown to you.

A word of caution about search engine research: Don't spend a lot of time researching a symbol this way. You can spend inordinate amounts of time reading and gleaning and be on the wrong trail, majoring in the minors. It's easy when using a search engine to "stretch" the Lord's intended meaning and be on a wild-goose chase.

Consider Positive and Negative Meanings

Many symbols can have either a positive or a negative meaning, depending on the use in the dream. You'll notice many symbols in the Symbol Dictionary have both positive and negative possibilities.

Many dreams are filled with negative symbols. Sometimes we interpret dreams filled with negative symbols and contort them to have positive meanings. This is incorrect interpretation, which can't give the dreamer the right message the Lord is attempting to convey, and it won't bring healing. A few examples of this are:

- Man in black clothing—this can't be correctly interpreted as a positive symbol. Wearing black clothing next to one's heart is a negative symbol and can mean death, famine, lack, or sin.

- Having sex with one's father—this is a negative symbol and can't be correctly viewed to be a positive one. The Lord wouldn't use an incestuous act to represent a positive meaning.

When we stretch a symbol to mean something positive when it's clearly a negative symbol, it can show a mindset unwilling to hear correction. Remember, He loves you and wants to correct your path and heal you.

People, Colors, and Places Are Big Keys

People in your dreams, especially those you know, are important keys and the first symbol to figure out in order to understand the correct meaning of dreams. Normally a person in your dream symbolizes a part of you.

It isn't the way of the Lord to reveal secrets about another person. Dreams are generally meant for you, the dreamer, not for the person who shows up in your dream. At rare times, a dream has a message to give another person; however, this is an unusual occurrence and it is always safer to assume the dream is about you first. Having interpreted thousands of dreams for many people, this is often the biggest mistake I see. It's also the one that can cause the most trouble with others, and what has often given dreams a bad rap in the Church as a whole. We'll address how to tell if your dream is for someone else in Chapter Eight, but I encourage you to try to interpret people in your dreams as symbolic for a part of you or your life.

So, how to know what people in your dreams mean? Let's look at some examples, beginning with the following ones from the Symbol Dictionary, the last chapter of this book.

- **Children:** *One's own children often mean what they symbolize to you.* For example, my grown children symbolize what they have recently gone through in their own lives, especially when I find myself dealing with similar issues.

- **Grandchild:** *Natural grandchild; heir; inheritance, including one's destiny or God's plan.* Recently I had the first dream of my granddaughter who is three-years-old at the time of this writing. She represents my inheritance, my destiny. My eleven-month-old granddaughter can symbolize the youngest, most immature part of me.

- **Mother:** *Church; one's job; one's natural mother; origin of a thought or idea.* When I dream of my own mother, she symbolizes the most mature part of me. At times, she can mean I'm dealing with fear, because she did. Think about what your mother struggled with as you consider your dream's meaning.

- **Father:** *God; apostle; pastor; one's own father.* For some of you, your dad could represent God; however, my dad accepted the Lord only a couple of years before he died and was still young in spiritual matters. Instead, the Spirit uses a pastor friend of mine as a symbol of Father God.

To discover what a person is symbolizing in your dreams, think about the different things they could mean to you. In dreams, they don't represent a general thing, like friendly, nice, sweet, etc. These are the answers most often given when a dreamer first tries to explain what a person means to them.

Instead, *the person likely symbolizes the issues the dreamer has in common with that person.* The Lord is working with us through symbols to get at heart issues, often at what is wrong with us rather than what is right, so consider the past or current issues with which that person struggles. Let's look at some examples:

- You could dream of a guy with whom you worked in the past who has serious insecurity issues. This would likely indicate you have struggled with your own insecurity issues during the last day or two in an exact situation. He would represent that part of you in the dream.

- Sometimes a person is used in a dream because of their name. If you dream about a friend of yours named "Patsy," for example, you are easily manipulated or taken advantage of in a particular situation since that's the definition of a "patsy." Last names can be used the same way. For instance, your friend named "Mike Steele" could be used to represent a thief (steal), even though he isn't one.

- When a name is symbolically used, the name will be in the dream, not just the person's appearance.

- At times, a person's name is interchangeable for another person of the same name. You might have a friend named Mike with whom you currently have problems and dream of an old friend from your high school days whose name is also Mike. In this case, your old friend Mike would represent your current friend Mike. Remember, the dream isn't likely showing you what's wrong with Mike, but your feelings, actions or reactions in the bothersome situation.

- When you dream of your pastor or other Christian leadership, they can represent good things, such as the Lord or their particular ministry position. Negatively, they can symbolize religious spirits working in your own life, since they are religious figures. Consider their clothing and actions in the dream to determine if they are being used as a positive or negative symbol. Even if they are being used as a negative symbol, this doesn't necessarily mean they are negative or religious in their real life. The dream is about the issues of the dreamer, not those of the characters in the dream.

- Prophets such as Rick Joyner or Jane Hamon could show up in your dreams to represent matters in the prophetic arena. These dreams likely aren't for them, their church or ministry; consider they are for you, although they could be prophesying to you in the dream. However, if the dream has symbols, you must find the correct interpretation to get a full understanding of the dream's correct meaning.

When you figure out what a person symbolizes, you will usually know what the dream is addressing, and then the rest of the dream begins to make sense.

Colors

The second important element that helps you more quickly understand the correct meaning of your dreams is the color that you or other people are wearing. The color of one's clothing that covers their heart, such as a shirt or sweater, indicates the condition of their heart about the situation the dream is addressing.

Colors also regularly come into play as interpretive signals for vehicles, such as cars, boats, buses, airplanes, and trains.

Colors also can have opposite meanings, depending on what is happening in the dream. For example, look at *white* from the Symbol

Dictionary:

> **White:** *Purity; righteousness; good deeds. However, a person dressed in white in the dream who is doing bad things often symbolizes a religious spirit.*
>
> *She [the bride of Christ] has been given the finest of pure white linen to wear. For the fine linen represents the good deeds of God's holy people (Revelation 19:8 NLT).*
>
> *Even Satan disguises himself as an angel of light (2 Corinthians 11:14 NLT).*

When you have a dream of someone wearing a white shirt, ask yourself and the Lord if you have been religious about a matter in the last couple of days. Do you know the person wearing the white shirt? If so, what do they symbolize to you? What root or branch meaning of *white* seems to fit the situation with which they've struggled? Do they tend to be religious or legalistic, or someone with a pure heart who is trying to live righteously?

If the person wearing the shirt is a "dream person," meaning a character that appears in your dream but not a person you know in real life, what are their words or actions in the dream? Are they positive or negative actions?

However, if you are the person in the dream wearing a white shirt, it's likely it indicates purity of heart about the dream's issue.

At times you or another person, whether a person known to you or not, can be wearing a white shirt and a different colored jacket. The color next to the heart—white—indicates a pure heart about the issue the dream is addressing, but the jacket's color gives you further insight. In such a case, combine the meanings.

For example, recently I met two young men, Paul and Evan, who regularly ministered to the homeless and drug addicts with a "bridge" ministry—they met under a bridge where the people lived.

Every weekend, they took food, clothing, blankets, and basic medical supplies to those who came to the meetings. The Holy Spirit showed up powerfully in the meetings, and many broken, hurting people received salvation, deliverance, and healing. They witnessed miracles on a regular basis, and then suddenly their main donor had a financial crisis, which caused the bridge ministry's finances to be extremely sparse.

Paul had a small part-time job and did all the work to get more donations for the food, clothing, and other items for the homeless. For this work, he was paid a salary from the ministry, but he had not received a paycheck for a month, and some of his bills were not being paid. Evan worked full-time and simply went to the bridge a few times a week to minister and help Paul.

Although Paul trusted the Lord, his situation was becoming bleak. The guys were considering cutting work time with the ministry, maybe even closing it down, so Paul could get a full-time job as well. During this time, Paul had a dream in which he was wearing a white tee shirt and a black sweater.

The white shirt symbolized his pure heart and trust for the Lord underneath the troublesome situation, because *white* was next to his heart. However, the black (meaning, in this case, lack) sweater showed he was striving and sweating about the situation.

The Lord wanted him to realize he was striving. The Lord's yoke is easy; He doesn't bring stress. The dream didn't give him an answer to his situation; it was addressing one topic—stress.

Places

The third element to help you quickly find the situation a dream is addressing is its setting. Look at the following examples.

- If a dream takes place at your home (meaning the setting of your dream, not the place in which you fell asleep and then had the dream), then the dream is dealing with your heart about a matter since we are the temple (home) of the Holy Spirit.

- If the setting is a friend's home, the meaning will be the same as if that person is in your dream. In other words, "you are in their home," means your actions, and your attitude about a matter is like theirs. It's not telling you anything about that person; the dream is about you.

- Should you have a dream about your grandparents' home, it could be addressing generational issues, such as addictions, curses, sins, or generational blessings, godly inheritance—your destiny. It could mean your actions and heart in a situation were like theirs, which is more likely to occur if you knew them well. It could be referring to your past or to a situation that happened in their home when you were younger. Consider all options when interpreting.

- When a dream is set in your church, or a church, a large airplane, train or bus, or a restaurant or cafeteria (we are fed spiritually at church), it's addressing a ministry and a situation that occurred in connection with church in the last couple of days. It could even be your reaction to something you heard on Christian television or a conversation you had with a friend about church. It can also represent your life since we are temples (churches) of the Holy Spirit.

He Often Speaks in Puns or Slang

Sometimes there are very "punny" things in a dream. I've found the Lord often speaks in slang. One example of this is when you have a dream like the following common one:

> "I dreamed I used a toilet in the middle of the mall. I had terrible diarrhea, walked away, and didn't flush it."

Diarrhea in a dream is often symbolic for "diarrhea of the mouth," gross I know, but slang for talking too much or feeling you have been too vulnerable with others and exposed yourself by things you said. It's strange to think that a holy God would talk like this, isn't it? Well, He does. He often speaks in parables, riddles, and dark sayings.

He Speaks about What's on Your Mind

The Lord often uses a topic that's on our mind as a teaching tool, a natural springboard from which to teach a spiritual principle. In Mark 8:15, as Jesus and His disciples were crossing the sea, the disciples suddenly remembered they had forgotten to bring bread. Jesus said, *"...Beware of the leaven of the Pharisees and Sadducees."* The disciples thought He spoke of leaven because they had forgotten bread, but it had nothing to do with that. He used those things on their minds in their natural life to teach them something spiritual.

He does the same thing in dreams. People often say things like, "I probably just had this dream about drowning because I was watching a movie last night and someone almost drowned in it." Because they had a similar experience hours before the dream, they think the dream is meaningless; however, the Lord uses the things on our minds and the symbols in our dreams (as he used *drowning* in the above dream) to tell us a spiritual principle, just like Jesus did in Mark 8:15.

Keys Points in This Chapter:

- Symbols are a type of figurative language used in Scripture and most other ways in which God speaks. This kind of language speaks to our hearts more than our logical minds.

- The meaning of the first appearance in Scripture of a word, color, number, name, or other term shows its basic, root meaning.

We can then apply that same idea of its use to other portions of Scripture and other ways God speaks, including dreams.

- God speaks the same language in dreams, visions, prophecy, and Scripture, although Scripture carries far more weight and certainty.

- Many symbols can have either a positive or a negative meaning, depending on its use in the dream.

- Negative symbolism is common in dreams in which God is showing us our heart, in order to bring healing of some kind.

- Often a symbol's meaning will be slang or a pun.

- Most of the time, a dream addresses things currently on your mind, those concerns that bothered you during the day (or night) you had the dream.

- People who appear as characters in your dream likely symbolize issues that you, the dreamer, have in common with that person. The dream is most always not about them.

- Three categories of symbols that are the most important to try to interpret are first—people, second—colors, and third—places.

CHAPTER SIX

Other Keys for Interpreting

This chapter is full of keys that will be helpful as you interpret your dreams, or those of others.

Yesterday Not Tomorrow

The single largest key the Lord has given me for dreams is that most of them are dealing with issues that occurred during the last day or two in the dreamer's life. Because some dreams in the Bible seem to deal with future, we tend to think of ours as future. According to Job 33, God often gives us dreams for the purpose of correction and healing. Through hearing and interpreting thousands of dreams, I've learned that *often* means *practically all the time.*

If you view your dreams as a course correction caused by events that occurred mostly either a day or two before you had the dream, rather than something you expect to happen in the future, you will see a huge shift in understanding, interpretation, and application. You will begin to see how He speaks most often in dreams about what's on our hearts and minds; you will draw closer to Him and your heart will be clearer.

Interpretation Should Be Soon

There isn't a dream in Scripture that was interpreted a long time after the dream occurred. In every case, the dream was interpreted the next day. This is another indication that many dreams are about circumstances occurring now in your life. After weeks, months, or more, one can't remember the difficulties that happened on the day of the dream, so it's usually impossible to interpret them correctly.

Write the Dream and Underline Symbols

As soon as possible after waking, write your dream and underline the symbols. It's a great idea to keep a notebook in which you write only dreams and other things you feel the Lord has spoken.

After writing the entire dream, underline the symbols—people, colors, places, things, actions, and numbers—then write what you think they mean. (For help with symbols, refer to the Symbol Dictionary, which lists many typical symbols you'll find in dreams, and Chapter Five, which contains keys to help you figure out what other symbols could mean.)

The following example shows how this works using a recent dream I had (We'll get more into this in Chapter Seven):

> I dreamed I was at <u>Mom's house,</u> and she was <u>cleaning</u> up the <u>kitchen</u> for the night because it was <u>bedtime</u>. I was in the <u>hallway</u> and saw the <u>back door, located in the kitchen,</u> suddenly <u>slam shut</u>, seemingly by itself.

The scene changed. I was still in the hallway but Mom was now there too. She had <u>closed the door</u> between the kitchen and the hall and <u>locked</u> it, rather than go back into the kitchen and lock the back door that had frightened her. <u>Afraid</u>, she had run into the hall. I said, "Mom, I saw the door close. It's OK. As a matter of fact, I'll go into the kitchen and lock those doors myself."

When I opened the hallway door, I saw the back door had now swung completely <u>open</u> to the outside, which caused concern. I could tell Mom would be frightened it had opened so wide, and I wondered who opened it.

I <u>pulled the back door closed</u> and the moment I was going to lock it, I felt a sudden twinge of <u>fear</u> and locked it very quickly. I looked to my left and Mom was back in the kitchen, locking other doors. She had felt <u>brave</u> after I made the first move and went into the kitchen to lock the back door.

Write the Symbol Meanings

- Mom's house—my mature part; my mom dealt with a spirit of fear, so the part of me that deals with fear.

- Cleaning—I think this means deliverance in this case, because of the numerous references to fear.

- Kitchen—the heart of the matter; my heart issues.

- Hallway—a place of transition; I am in much transition currently.

- Back door—the past; generational issues, Mom dealt with fear.

- Slammed shut—something caused a door to the past issue to close.

- Closed the door to the kitchen—looks like this dream deals with generational issues of fear; a part of me is running away from fear rather than dealing with it (Mom running due to fear symbolizes my current running from something due to fear. She represents me.).

- Lock those doors myself—I made a decision to deal with the situation.

- Door had swing wide open to the outside—the door was wide open again.

- I felt fear and locked the door—since I felt fear in the dream as well as other symbols indicate fear, there is no doubt the topic of the dream is fear. At least I did get the door locked finally.

- Mom was also locking doors—the part of me that deals with fear overcame it and locked it out.

Many symbols in this particular dream are repetitive. There is no need to write the same symbol and its meaning numerous times.

Read the Meaning of the Symbols like a Story

Following the storyline through the symbolic meanings often gives an idea of the issue the dream is addressing. In this dream, you can read and think through the meanings for the symbols and see a slightly different storyline emerge. You will sometimes begin to understand the figurative picture the dream is presenting.

Often the storyline itself is in figurative language, which means that words or expressions are used in a metaphorical rather than literal way. In this dream, the focus of the storyline was symbolic: doors were being locked and swinging back open, meaning I was both standing against an issue (by locking it out) and the issue kept plaguing my mind (swinging back open).

This dream deals with my fear while I'm in a place of transition, which in my case means dealing with the unknown future. It's also easy to see that this fear is a generational issue in my family.

Using the above dream as an example, here's how to read the meaning of the symbols like a storyline:

> Either my mature part, or the part of me that deals with fear like Mom did, was trying to get deliverance from some heart issue while I'm in this place of transition. The door to fear kept opening and closing, and it seemed it was doing it on its own, which could mean I didn't really do anything to cause this. I tried to get it closed and locked.

And with that, I immediately knew exactly the issue the dream was dealing with.

Look for People, Places, and Colors

People known to you that show up in your dreams are often the most important keys on which to focus to find the correct meaning of a dream. Focus on the meaning of those symbols first.

In the above dream, my mom represents the part of me that struggles with certain issues pertaining to fear. Since fear appears numerous times, it's clear this is the topic addressed in the dream.

Pray

Even though the Lord doesn't normally give you easy answers to the meanings of your dreams, He will help you solve them. At this point, ask Him to open your heart and understanding to discover what He wants you to know. Ask Him to help you think in figurative language and to convict your heart about the issue He's addressing in the dream.

Then meditate on what you see in writing rather than the feeling you were experiencing *as a reaction* to the dream when you wake up. Some dreams are very graphic and your feelings about them can confuse your ability to interpret them correctly. It's far easier to understand a correct interpretation when the dream is in writing, like a story, rather than when you are "living it" in the dream and have an emotional reaction.

Conversely, the feeling you have *in* a dream can be an indicator of the dream's meaning.

As I meditated on the dream above, I saw the door to fear was closing and opening but I finally locked it. The dream addressed my actions in an exact situation that occurred the day before I had the dream. When I prayed about the dream, I closed the door to a generational spirit that had triggered fear in my situation.

> *For God has not given us the spirit of fear, but of power, and of love, and of a sound mind (2 Timothy 1:7 KJV).*

Think about Yesterday's Events

This is another big key. If you think through what happened during the day or evening and try to remember events or thoughts that gave you a feeling other than peace—a tightening in your gut, a quick retort, sudden anger, an over-reaction—you will likely have a clue what the dream is about before beginning to interpret it.

During the night, before the dream, I had thoughts about how difficult it would be to make the transition to which the Lord was appointing me. I was surprised to be having such thoughts because many times in the past, He's called me to "walk on water" and always held me up when I did. These thoughts of fear were surprising, and I quickly struggled to get control of them.

My mom wanted life to be steady, safe, and secure. She would choose to be in the boat rather than chance sinking, and my thoughts were like hers in that situation. For a few minutes, I was afraid for the future and considered whether to look for more security. However, the

Lord hasn't called me to a life of staying in the boat. I have a history with Him, and I trust His plan for my future. The dream above addressed these thoughts as I struggled with both sides of the issue (the door opening and closing).

Follow the Thread

As you meditate on the storyline in the dream, you might start to see something that reminds you of a situation that happened yesterday, the day before, or in the last few days.

You will often see something in the written dream that begins to make sense, like a puzzle piece that seems to fit. I call this a "thread," like finding an end in a tangled bunch of rope. You can then follow the rest of the symbols to find the dream's topic.

The "thread," in the dream above, was easy to find. A few different symbols, as well as a feeling of fear in the dream, indicated I was dealing with issues of fear. A feeling experienced *in* a dream can be an indicator of a dream's meaning, while an emotional reaction *to* the dream upon waking usually isn't.

Be Careful of a Stretch

Be careful of what I call a "stretch." That's when one assigns extra meaning to a symbol when the dots aren't there to connect it. Keep the interpretation and application as simple as possible.

For example, in the story about my dream of Mom, it would be a stretch to consider the dream's intended meaning was that my dad had opened the door to fear in our lives because he didn't submit his life to the Lord. Dad wasn't in the dream, and there was no insinuation of him in it.

It would also be a stretch to consider the dream indicated that the enemy was attempting to break in to my church, or the Church as a whole.

There are no symbols of the Church in the dream. Even though as prophetic people, some of the issues with which we struggle are the same issues the Church is battling, the great majority of our dreams are for us only.

Dreams Can Address Your Thoughts

My dream above was about a mental struggle I had during the night, not necessarily a wrong action or reaction. The Lord is interested in every little thing about you. Even when you hide your feelings from others, or choose not to react in a tough situation, He sees your every thought and inward struggle. It's been surprising to see how many dreams deal with a dreamer's inward battle and thoughts, rather than their outward actions or reactions.

Thoughts trigger feelings. Resentment or offense can grow in our hearts when we stifle emotions. As we discussed in Chapter One, sometimes these inward reactions cause sicknesses such as arthritis, cancer, and autoimmune diseases.

The best response to a tough situation isn't a bad reaction, and it isn't stuffing down our emotions. Jesus did neither, and we are each in a process, being transformed into His image. He told us to forgive one another—from our hearts—endless times, to prefer one another, and to love the Lord and other people.

He knew that mankind was a dysfunctional mess and needed a Savior and transformation. The transformation process begins at salvation, the moment we accept Jesus in our heart, and ends at our death. In the meantime, the Lord addresses our thoughts, actions, and reactions in many ways, including dreams.

These Things Take Time

Usually it takes a period of time, more than a few minutes, to understand a dream's correct meaning. It just can't be rushed. You must sit quietly and meditate on it as you bring it to the Lord. This takes practice. Dream interpretation is an art, not a science.

Like learning a new language (which this is), it takes time, practice, and patience. When you give it enough time, you can often begin to see a thread in the story line or in one or more of the symbols and find the dream's meaning.

When the Issue is Resolved in the Dream

It seemed the issue was resolved in the dream above—I locked the door and Mom locked the other doors. Logic would say the situation was handled, and the question then would be, "If the issue was resolved, why did I have a dream about the situation?"

The answer is that it wasn't totally resolved, or He wouldn't have spoken in symbols. Symbols indicate that something is unclear to the dreamer or something is wrong in the dreamer's mind, heart, or emotions. Notice that close to the end of that dream, the very instant I closed the door to lock it, I felt a twinge of fear, even though I locked the door.

You must be vulnerable, honest, and introspective to find a correct interpretation. The Lord will increase your capacity for these traits as you try to interpret your dreams.

Why Can't I Just Ask the Lord for the Interpretation?

When I was first experiencing many dreams every night, a mentor told me he believed dream interpretation worked like a supernatural prayer language—you simply ask for the interpretation, open your mouth, and out it will come. That would be so easy for us, but that process would totally bypass the Lord's reason for speaking in symbols.

He does speak to us about the issue the dream addresses, however. Actually, He speaks to us about it once or twice, before we have the dream. He makes it easy for us at the beginning of a troublesome situation, and speaks in a variety of ways, warning, convicting, and instructing us against our intended actions or reactions.

If we don't hear Him because our hearts are calloused in that particular area, or we refuse to obey Him, He has no choice but to make it harder for us. His intention is to transform us into the image of Jesus, who always heard Him because His heart was pure and always obeyed Him. In order to transform us, we must change, and we often learn through our mistakes.

Since most dreams deal with our intentions and mindsets, He uses symbols to bypass them. It's hard to hear Him when our minds are made up about a matter. He doesn't often simply speak the interpretation to a Job 33/Symbolic dream, but requires us to search our own hearts, as well as His, to discover where we have gotten off the path.

The Bible states, *It is the glory of God to conceal a thing but it is the honor of kings to search out a matter (Proverbs 25:2 KJV).* He hides some things from us on purpose so we will seek Him.

One Central Theme

Each dream has one central theme. When correctly interpreted, every symbol can be applied toward the theme and its meaning. The Lord doesn't change ideas in the middle of a dream and then address a different issue. If you cannot interpret the majority of the dream, you should assume you might be on the wrong track about the interpretation. One part of the dream might seem understandable, but if you don't get the exact topic of the idea He is presenting, you could be taking it opposite of His intention.

Dreams have only one meaning, not layers of meaning like Scripture can have. When interpreting dreams, if at first we have one understanding and later another, we must determine the correct interpretation. It's not both.

One Subject at a Time

At times, He doesn't speak in symbols, but in clear language. The words He speaks at these times tend to be profound secrets.

> Years ago, I was fasting and praying with questions about interpretation of dreams and prophetic words. One night, I awoke around 3 A.M., got out of bed, and groped through the dark with absolutely nothing on my mind as I plodded half-asleep from the bed to the bathroom. I heard Him speak. His words were clear, loud, and precise, "Whenever I speak, whether it's in a dream, prophecy, vision, or in Scripture, I am addressing one topic at a time."
>
> Stunned with the suddenness and clarity of His voice, which seemed to be audible, I stopped in my tracks and spoke something stupid aloud in response. "Lord," I said, "Now, You know me. You know I'm going to have to see that in the Word."
>
> "Fine," He said, "Joel, Amos, Obadiah." And with that, He was gone.
>
> Taken aback, I went to the kitchen table with my Bible and looked up the books He had just mentioned, which were next to one another in the order He had spoken them. For the next few weeks, I studied and found each book to be about one topic, one central theme, although each theme was viewed differently from chapter to chapter.
>
> This principle has become a guide and invaluable tool as I interpret dreams and all other revelation, even Scripture. He is a God of order, and He speaks on one topic until He has said what He intends to say about that subject at that time.

Specific Not General

Another important key when interpreting is to think in specific terms. Dreams address a specific issue, not general ones. If you think in terms such as, "I believe the Lord is telling me that whenever I..." or other general terms, that's not likely the right interpretation. Look for the exact situation that occurred a day or two ago, not a general idea, to correctly pinpoint the issue so you can properly apply the interpretation and get the dream's full benefit.

For example, my dream with Mom appearing as a character was addressing fear, but not all fear in my life. It was addressing one specific issue. I had awakened during the night with extremely fearful thoughts, about a specific and current issue pertaining to my own future in a way I've never dealt with before. I knew it was unusual for me to have such thoughts about an area of my life where I've always had faith. I intensely struggled with the thoughts for a few minutes, going back and forth between faith and fear. At the end of the mental battle, I was approaching a place of faith and trying to trust the Lord to take care of those issues, as He always has. After the mental struggle, I fell back asleep and had the dream.

The dream addressed a specific issue about fear—the mental battle I had during the night—not all kinds of fear. He wanted to correct my way of thinking and struggle about that exact issue, and He wanted to heal my heart and mind from fearful thoughts about that situation.

Most Dreams Are for the Dreamer, Not for the Church

I acknowledge there are those who have a gifting of having dreams for the Church at large, for leadership, and for others. At times, I hear such dreams; on rare occasions I have one myself. As prophetic people, our lives, and therefore our dreams, can be signs of what the Lord is doing on a large scale or of situations the Church is experiencing.

70

Sometimes we are given such dreams, but again, it's not the norm. Usually the dreams for the Church or leadership are of a different pattern than one filled with symbols that require interpretation, or else the meaning of the symbols is relatively obvious, or sometimes the Lord or an angel gives the interpretation in the dream.

The safe position is to understand that, with exceptions, dreams are for the one who dreams them. When we believe our dreams are for the Church at large, our local church, leadership, or other people, we are often missing the point the Lord is trying to make.

Since His intention with many dreams is to bypass our wrong mindset and/or correct our path to keep us from the enemy's plans, we must view our dreams from that perspective before assuming they are for others. The bottom line is this: we don't want to get sick; we need to view most dreams as though He wants to speak to us about our heart issues.

Reoccurring Dreams

The time between similar dreams matters. There is a huge difference in God's purposes between similar dreams that occur over a long time period and similar dreams you have in a short period of time. The difference is the timeline.

When the Lord has established a situation to happen, you can have two or more similar dreams in one night, or maybe during two or three nights. These dreams can have an element of foretelling.

Dreams that seem similar but occur weeks, months, or years apart, point to a different purpose. These dreams can address an issue with which you've dealt for a time, even a long time, but you haven't effectively overcome it. You keep having the issue, so you keep having the dream, or a similar dream. Reoccurring symbolic dreams are not foretelling; they are Job 33/Symbolic dreams and deal with the issue(s) of your heart.

Nightmares

Both Job and Nebuchadnezzar said their dreams from the Lord were "terrifying." There isn't a dream in the Bible that is from a source other than the Lord. None of them were credited to overeating, being sick, tired, or from the enemy.

Perhaps there are some terrifying dreams that are from the enemy if the dreamer's heart, mind, and spirit belong to him; I can't say. I haven't heard any of those dreams.

Some dreams are graphic and upsetting; it's hard to think they could be from the Lord. Dreams address our spiritual state; it helps to remember the graphics are symbolic, not literal.

There are times the Lord opens our eyes and ears as we sleep, so that we are able to recognize the enemy's strategies against us. In these cases, it is the Lord's grace to reveal these matters to us. He does this so we can repent to get our hearts and minds clean, forgive those who have hurt us, and then cast out the enemy.

Myths and Misinterpretations

Let's look at commonly believed myths that can throw you off track of the Lord's intentions in giving you the dream. Sometimes, it helps to learn what to do by knowing what not to do.

My Dreams Foretell the Future like Those in the Bible

Some of the dreams in the Bible are foretelling, but some bring correction, instruction, or warning. Job 33:29 tells us God often gives us corrective dreams, and those are the type of dreams most of us regularly experience. As we study Scriptural dreams, we see correction as one of the Lord's intentions in many of them, even some with foretelling aspects.

A popular view of dream interpretation today is that most are foretelling a future event. Dreamers do still have some dreams that tell of future events, though the fact is those dreams are not nearly as common as are those of the Job 33/Symbolic pattern. After interpreting thousands of dreams for hundreds of people, I found only about a handful were foretelling. However, we will cover other patterns in later chapters to be able to differentiate between types of dreams and to recognize a foretelling dream when one is given.

If I Remember the Dream, it's from God

There are those who believe a dream is from God only if they remember it vividly. However, Nebuchadnezzar had an important dream showing correction for himself, and end-time prophetic revelation, and didn't remember it.

There are certain dreams that do stand out more than others do. At times, it could be the Lord causing us to remember them more vividly.

Science has learned that whether we remember a dream or not has to do with the sleep-state we are in when we have the dream.

There are seasons in our lives when we remember more dreams than other times. There is a certain grace the Lord gives at times to remember dreams, but that doesn't mean to pay attention to only those.

Years ago, I was "pounding heaven" for a better remembrance of my dreams upon waking. They do tend to slip away like a feather floating by, don't they? During that time, I had a dream about trying to remember my dreams better.

I dreamed I awakened and couldn't remember my dream. I closed my eyes and fervently cried for remembrance. Suddenly the dream popped into my mind.

A few days later, I tried the dream's direction (to fervently ask for remembrance) when I awoke and knew I'd had a dream but couldn't remember it. It worked; I remembered my dream!

The Bible tells us, *The effective, fervent prayer of a righteous man avails much (James 5:16).* The Greek word *energoumenē* is translated as effective or fervent. According to the Greek Lexicon, it means *very hard work.* It also can mean *energize, to work in a situation to take it from one stage to the next.* When we fervently pray, we create the spiritual energy to make changes.

So, I encourage you to pray fervently to remember your dreams.

If the Dream Has Color, it's from God

Some dreamers consider a black-and-white dream to be unimportant yet one with vivid color to be from God, but this is an incorrect, unsubstantiated correlation.

It Was Just a Dream

If you learn to interpret your dreams according to the principles in this book, I believe you'll agree that dreams are spiritual communication. They are an important way the Lord speaks to mankind. None of them are "just dreams." As it states in Joel, we are truly in an age of God pouring his dreams, and other revelation, upon us.

Symbols Are Specific to Each Person

Many symbols in the dreams of young children, old men, young women, Asian, Black, or Caucasian, mean the same thing to everyone. There are some symbols that will be specific to an individual, such as what individual people symbolize or items specific to a certain culture. Symbols that are slang can also speak to people differently, as one generation or culture may not understand a saying popular with another group.

However, since dreams are mostly given in God's language, not ours, many symbols are universal.

What Dreams Aren't Saying

The following topics are common in dreams and are very rarely foretelling, though some dreamers erroneously understand them to be. Expect these subjects to be symbolic when they appear in your dreams.

- Marriage: Although not impossible, it's not likely that your dreams tell you whom to marry. The Lord gave us free will, and although He leads us in all decisions, He doesn't often give us this kind of information in a dream. If you believe He is telling you this, please do yourself a huge favor and consult with a few mature believers before you attach faith to this kind of dream. "Marrying" someone, in symbolic language, means coming into intimate agreement with what that person represents. See *Marriage* in the Symbol Dictionary at the back of this book.

- Death: It's also unlikely a dream is telling you someone (including you) will die, although like marriage dreams it can happen at times. This is quite rare and can't be trusted to be His direction. Attaching faith to a death "foreseen" in a dream would take much more confirmation. He has spoken to me about the deaths of a few who have been close and important to me, though He spoke those things to me clearly in my heart rather than in a dream.

  When we dream of someone's death in the midst of a symbolic dream, most likely that person symbolizes a part of us that "died" in a situation the day or so before the dream. These kinds of dreams can be awful to experience. At times, we dream of one of our children dying, and it feels like too much to bear emotionally. Again, our children in these cases are often symbolic for a part of us. See *Children* and *Death* in the Symbol Dictionary.

For an extreme example, a twenty-six year old woman named Susan had married young, and her husband was physically violent. He cheated on her numerous times during their one-year marriage. She filed for divorce, and, when I met her, she weighed only eighty-five pounds due to the intense trauma and heartbreak. Sobbing and scared, she told me a vivid, horrific dream in which she had died and was being buried on a cold, gray, dreary day. Her spirit was lingering and hovering above her grave, and she could see her husband and his girlfriend, arms around one another, at her funeral. The pain of seeing them together was heartbreaking. She thought the dream was telling her that, on top of everything else she was suffering, she would soon die.

However, the symbolism meant this: Susan had been through such great emotional trauma that a part of her had completely emotionally "died." I was able to assure her the dream was not addressing her death, and, with the help of counselors and family, she began to pull out of the severe trauma.

- Pregnancy: It's also probable that your dreams are not foretelling an actual pregnancy. Even men have dreams of being pregnant! Pregnancy in dreams symbolizes an idea or thought of something new going on in your life; you are "pregnant" with a new business idea, for example. The pregnancy could symbolize something good or bad.

- Accidents: Dreams aren't apt to be revealing an impending accident. An accident symbolizes an altercation with another person that happened a day or two prior to the dream, and sometimes in the past. A dreamer saying, "I hit a car head-on," would mean they harshly confronted another person in their natural life, likely the day before the dream.

- Presidential Dreams: It's doubtful your dreams tell you anything bad about the president or that he is about to be assassinated. Usually the president symbolizes a person that has authority in your life, such as your husband, boss, pastor, or others. At times, the president symbolizes a part of you that is bossing and controlling others.

  If the dream is in symbols, it isn't saying a person will literally be assassinated. When we dream there is a plot to kill someone, it usually means we have "killed" someone with our words, or it speaks of our hatred for them, or we have been thinking of how we could take revenge against them.

- Secrets or Sins of Another: One of the most important things I want to tell you is that dreams aren't about the secrets or the sin of another person, even though they appear as a character in your dream.

  God doesn't normally give you prophetic words for others in a dream, nor tell you their secrets or sins, with a rare exception—when you have a heart for that person and sincerely want to help them, and He knows when you truly do or not. There have only been two dreams in my experience, in which the Lord revealed the issues of another person in a dream, and in both instances, it was a close family member of the dreamer. The Lord gave the dream both times so the dreamer would know how to pray, and how to handle a relationship with the family member in a more productive way.

  Other people usually represent a part of you, the part you have in common with them in a specific area with which you are dealing at the time of the dream.

Pizza Dreams

Eating complex carbohydrates at night, such as pizza, can influence dreaming. Going to bed with a tummy full of bread will cause you to go into a deep-sleep state easily. Science believes more dreams happen during deep-sleep stages, so you will have more dreams if you are full. So there could be something to the term *pizza dreams*, but that doesn't discount them from any other dream patterns. You might have more dreams when you eat pizza or heavy food, but they still have meaning.

Busy Dreams

> *Too much activity gives you restless dreams, too many words make you a fool (Ecclesiastes 5:3 NLT).*

The busier you are, the more issues you have. The more you must handle, the greater the chances you will mishandle some of it, so the more you'll dream. Interpretation is still necessary, and the same guidelines apply. There is no such thing as "busy dreams," meaning you can just discount them.

Now, let's get into the business of interpreting your dreams.

Key Points in This Chapter:

Most headings in this chapter are key points. Look back over those to review key points.

CHAPTER SEVEN

How to Interpret Your Job 33/ Symbolic Dreams *Tomorrow*

The following steps will be helpful to follow as you learn to interpret your symbolic dreams.

Step One: Write the Dream

The best way to begin to interpret a symbolic dream is to write it out as soon as possible after waking. Purchase a notebook in which to write your dreams and other revelation from the Lord and keep it by your bed. If you are getting many dreams and waking in the night, you might put an inexpensive digital voice recorder next to your bed to record them during the night, and then write them the next morning.

Step Two: Underline the Symbols

Read back over the dream and underline those words that are symbolic—people, colors, places, things, actions, and numbers—that appear in your dream. For example, look at the underlined symbols in this dream from Paul, a young man new to teaching a group:

> "I dreamed I was <u>cooking</u> dinner for my <u>friends</u> at <u>church</u>. I was cooking <u>fried chicken</u> and <u>yellow squash</u>."

Step Three: Write the Symbols and Their Possible Meanings

Under the dream, write the symbols you underlined and their possible meanings. Refer to the Symbol Dictionary to help you get started, and to Chapter Five in this book for help interpreting symbols if a word is not in the dictionary. Here are some possible meanings for the symbols we underlined:

- Cooking—"feeding" others, teaching, prophesying, mentoring in some way
- Friends at church—some meeting, church, home group, talking about the Lord; thoughts of church
- Chicken—fear, afraid
- Yellow—again, fear
- Squash—feeling of being "squashed" or put down

Step Four: Look for People, Colors, Places

People: The people were "dream people," not anyone Paul knew or had ever seen, but they were "church people," which indicated they represented something that occurred at a meeting where the things of the Lord were being discussed or they symbolized the dreamer's thoughts about something church-related.

Colors: The color Paul remembered—yellow—indicated he was afraid.

Places: In this dream the place also speaks of a church meeting, same as the "church people," so it is a second indicator the dream was addressing an issue the dreamer was having that was church-related.

Step Five: Look for the Thread

After writing the symbols and their meanings, often a thread seems to appear that will give you a clue where to begin to interpret the dream. Sometimes the thread is in the feel of the storyline, and at times in one or more symbols.

It's easy to see a thread of a likely interpretation when you shift your thinking into figurative language rather than literal. Read through the symbols' meanings and see how they paint a word picture.

In Paul's dream, the thread is easy to find by reading through the meaning of the symbols: he was "feeding" others at a church meeting and was afraid of rejection.

In the dream, he was cooking friend chicken and yellow squash. We tend to think literally when learning to interpret dreams but almost all dreams are metaphorical, figurative language.

Step Six: Notes on Recent Events in Your Life

Often you won't get the interpretation immediately from writing the dream, underlining its symbols, and assigning meanings to them. The next step is to make some notes on those things that were bothering you the day or two before your dream.

Here are notes from the dreamer about the day before he had the above dream:

> "Last night, I taught at a home group. The information
> I was sharing was new to them and I struggled with

how to present it. I was afraid they would reject the message, and reject me too."

When you think of the dreamer's troublesome situation the night before, the topic and meaning of his dream becomes clearer.

Step Seven: Write the Interpretation and Application

Here is the application for the above dream: The dream dealt with his fear of rejection from the group. He's going to pray and ask the Lord to help him overcome a fear of rejection in this situation, because he feels called to teach.

This is the kind of dream that many would discount as "just a dream" while the Lord wants Paul to deal with his fear and forge ahead with his call to teach.

Examples: Symbolic Dreams—Job 33 Format

Healing From Panic Attacks

Jim, a young man from a church where I had ministered, called me one Sunday evening, very depressed. It seemed too much was going wrong in his life—although he was serving the Lord, he couldn't seem to find peace. There were problems at work, his mom had recently died, there were big issues with his roommate, and now constant panic attacks. I was listening quietly as he vented his pain, when suddenly he began to tell me a recent dream that captured my attention.

There were many details in the dream, and one part stood out: a certain old friend was in the dream. Since people we know that appear as characters in our dreams represent a specific trait or situation we have in common with them, I knew this was likely the thread on which to pull to find the answer to the dream's puzzle. When I asked for details about the old friend, all Jim could remember was they had gone to church together in the past, and the friend had stopped going when his girlfriend became pregnant.

The person in the dream likely symbolized someone having intimate relations but not married, since that was the outstanding quality about him to Jim. I carefully asked, "Are you sleeping with someone?" Blown away, his answer was "Yes, how did you know?" I knew because that's how it works with people in our dreams; they represent a part of us, an issue that we have in common with them at the time of our dream.

As we further talked about the pain and loneliness that had driven him to what he termed "casual intimacy," I remembered a part of Rick Joyner's book "The Call" in which Rick experienced several prophetic encounters. The one in mind was a conversation with Jonah, who said, "When you draw close [to the Lord] with hidden sin in your heart, it will drive you to insanity, as many have learned through the ages." I read that portion of the book to Jim and he knew his sin was the cause of his recent panic attacks. He repented, and the Lord healed him.

He has been delighted that God gave him the dream and welcomed the correction because it brought healing.

Deliverance from Alcoholism

Patty was such a pretty lady, always well dressed, with silky auburn hair, a ready smile, and easy laugh. She and her husband were home-group leaders and parents of a beautiful teen-aged daughter. They were the perfect picture of young Christians who you would think had life and their faith going for them in every way. She called one morning asking if we could meet, saying the Lord had sent her to me for deliverance from alcoholism.

She hadn't drunk alcohol in some time, she said, but the temptation was there every time a negative issue cropped up in her life. We prayed deliverance prayers from alcoholism and generational issues.

She sensed a great relief and hoped she was totally free but had nagging thoughts. *This is how my family is. We have alcohol issues. Am I really free?* That night she had a dream.

> "I dreamed I was with another person and we were hunting snakes. I looked out the door from my living room and saw two huge, dead snakes hung over a fence."

"When I woke up," she told me, "the sight of two such huge, ugly snakes was very frightening and my heart was racing, but when I wrote out the dream, I realized we had indeed killed the snakes of alcoholism and its generational hold on my life. I wasn't frightened at all then, but grateful to the Lord for the power of His blood and name. I'm free!"

The snakes in Patty's dream were generational issues of alcoholism and her own problems with addiction to it. The Lord corrected her thinking, letting her know He had delivered her from alcohol, so the enemy couldn't continue to plague her with thoughts of doubt. Without the dream, she could have fallen into a mindset that He hadn't answered her prayer, and could have begun drinking again whenever there were negative situations in her life. The dream was correcting her mindset and giving her encouragement to continue to be free of alcoholism.

> *As he [a man] thinketh in his heart, so he is (Proverbs 23:7 KJV).*

Ex-Husband Dream

Fran, a pretty, middle-aged, divorced Realtor, was a whole-hearted believer in Jesus, but struggled with life's issues. Her life hadn't been a bed of roses, and she found it difficult not to be angry and offended. She felt she had "tried and tried" but couldn't seem to get into a good frame of mind and stay there.

During a particularly hard time, when she had been fired from her job and was struggling to make ends meet, she was complaining because the Lord had not brought her a husband. Then she had this dream:

> "I dreamed I was remarrying Jeff, my ex-husband. Even though I didn't love him in the dream—or in reality either—I had agreed to marry him and was having sex with him. His hair was a mess and his face was deformed."

When I walked in to greet Fran, she immediately began to cry and ask, "Why would God want me to marry him again? He was mean to me. I don't understand; he remarried years ago, and although they aren't happy at all, am I to wait until he gets a divorce then remarry him? That would be even worse than things are now, but I'm willing to do whatever God wants me to do."

Fran was greatly relieved to know the dream didn't show God's plan for her to remarry Jeff. She laughed when she realized Jeff represented her "old man," her old nature, before she was born-again (Ephesians 4:22-24). (See the Symbol Dictionary.)

Looking at other symbols in her dream, her old man was a mess and "deformed," because it couldn't be made perfect in God's eyes.

As we all are, in different ways and degrees, Fran is in the Lord's process of learning to die to the old nature and come alive in the new nature that Jesus died for her to experience. Correctly interpreting and applying her dreams on a regular basis will help her accomplish much more in her sanctification process, and she will grow into a more intimate relationship with the Lord.

Key Points in This Chapter:

- There are eight basic steps that will help you interpret your dreams:

1. Write the dream.

2. Underline the symbols.

3. Write the symbols and possible meanings.

4. Ask the Lord for His wisdom and guidance.

5. Look for people, colors, and places.

6. Look for the thread.

7. Make notes on recent events in your life.

8. Write the interpretation and application.

CHAPTER EIGHT

Understanding and Interpreting All Other Patterns

A Voice or Appearance of an Angel or the Lord

Dreams of the second pattern, a Voice or Appearance of an Angel or the Lord, tend to be clear and specific rather than symbolic. When you experience one of these dreams, you might see an angel or the Lord or you might not see anything at all, but you definitely hear a voice. The dreams in Scripture of this pattern are clear, specific, and rarer than symbolic ones. They were then, and are now, for warning and/or instruction, and like Job 33/Symbolic dreams, some of them can bring a form of correction. However, this kind of dream has a greater possibility of being foretelling, bringing warning, or giving instruction than symbolic ones. They are clear and usually need no interpretation.

The voice of the Lord or an angel tends to be louder and clearer when we sleep than when we're awake. Some dreams of this pattern can be "taken to the bank" to be the Lord's warning or instruction.

Still, we must apply active faith, praying and acting in agreement with what He has shown to be His will or against impending judgment, to do our part as His friends to whom He spoke clearly.

Consider, for instance, those dreams given to Mary's husband, Joseph: Four times the Lord gave him dreams with clear instruction or warning. The pattern was the same in each; there was no need for interpretation. The first one came to him in his sleep during the time he was shocked and very concerned that Mary was pregnant:

> *But after he had considered this, an angel of the Lord appeared to him in a dream and said, "Joseph son of David, do not be afraid to take Mary home as your wife, because what is conceived in her is from the Holy Spirit" (Matthew 1:20 NIV).*

Notice he pondered a particular question and the Lord answered him.

An angel appeared and spoke in the dream, which is an indication of warning or instruction.

There was correction of his fear.

No interpretation was necessary; there were no visuals and therefore no pictures in the dream. The dream was simply the voice of an angel or the Lord speaking clear instruction, with no symbols or riddles to interpret.

After the child was born and the wise men visited, Joseph had another dream of the same pattern. This one brought warning and instruction:

> *When they had gone, an angel of the Lord appeared to Joseph in a dream. "Get up," he said, "Take the child and*

his mother and escape to Egypt. Stay there until I tell you, for Herod is going to search for the child to kill him" (Matthew 2:13 NIV).

The third dream was of the same pattern—the appearance of an angel who brought clear instruction:

After Herod died, an angel of the Lord appeared in a dream to Joseph in Egypt and said, "Get up, take the child and his mother and go to the land of Israel, for those who were trying to take the child's life are dead" (Matthew 2:20 NIV).

The Lord carefully led Joseph with clear direction through dreams. No chances could be taken with the life and safety of Jesus, and the dreams didn't contain symbolism that could be misinterpreted.

Warning Dreams

Then he had a fourth dream of warning and instruction:

But when Joseph heard that Archelaus was reigning in Judea in place of his father Herod, he was afraid to go there. Having been warned in a dream, he withdrew to the district of Galilee, and he went and lived in a town called Nazareth. So was fulfilled what was said through the prophets, that he would be called a Nazarene (Matthew 2:22-23 NIV).

He was carefully led away from danger and into the right geographical area for God's purposes, through dreams that contained the appearance or voice of an angel.

Another interesting example is the dream in which the Lord spoke to king Abimilech:

You are as good as dead because of the woman you have taken. She is a married woman (Genesis 20:3 NIV).

This dream had no picture; it was the voice of the Lord or an angel, with a clear warning. There was no interpretation needed, and it was for warning.

This kind of dream, like Abimilech's dream and those of Mary's husband, Joseph, are true warning dreams.

A few years ago in October, the Lord spoke to me in my sleep with clear, specific instruction of where to move, what to do with my furniture, the kind of place to rent, what to do regarding business and ministry, and the month I was to go. Such exact leading is rare and I was cautious. I thought, *I know He said for me to move in April, but this is a huge move, and really, does He mean next April or another one in a future year?* So I put it on a back burner in my mind. Then in February, as I slept, an angel spoke to me loudly and awakened me.

"You're going to sit right here while the Lord is trying to get you out of here."

This was a clear warning. I had been told clearly what to do in October, but was afraid of making a prophetic mistake so did nothing. There was no picture and no symbols to interpret. He had indeed meant that specific April.

Clear Instruction from the Voice of the Lord in a Dream

Sometimes the Lord speaks clear, profound instruction in a dream. In the dream below, He gave direction for the way He wants me to invest client's assets to move into a Kingdom mindset.

"I want you to drill down into companies," He said, "and find out if the company was founded on Christian principles and if the present leadership tithe. I'm no longer going to bless the world; I will only bless Christian companies."

Like Solomon in the Bible, I responded in my sleep, "But Lord," I said, "It's been my experience that (1) Christian companies don't generally have the wisdom to make money, and (2) if they do, they rip you off worse than the world."

"RE-GARD-LESS," He sternly responded, "If you want to make a profit, you're going to have to invest in Christian companies." The way He had enunciated the word "regardless" felt like He was giving me a stern reprimand about my opinion of His decisions.

Emphatically He finished His message, "It's time for My people to put their money where their mouth is."

When you have a dream of this pattern, the information it contains can be trusted to be more reliable than a dream with symbols, which must be interpreted. Still, you must always test the spirits and be sure the words spoken align with all of God's counsel.

There are dreams that contain both symbols and the voice or appearance of the Lord or an angel. In these cases, the Lord is bringing true warning or foretelling as well as some kind of correction, because He is giving a part of the dream in symbols.

Friends of God

Scripture indicates the Lord sometimes speaks to us clearly rather than in symbols, riddles, or parables when we are intimate with Him. The Lord spoke clearly to Moses, for example:

> *The Lord would speak to Moses face to face, as a man speaks to a friend (Exodus 33:11 NIV).*

Aaron and Miriam had complained about Moses, and the Lord came down in the form of a pillar of cloud and spoke:

If there is a prophet among you, I, the Lord, will make Myself known to him in a vision, I will speak to him in a dream. Not so with my servant Moses, He is faithful in all My household. With him I speak mouth to mouth, even openly, not in riddles or dark sayings (Numbers 12:8 NAS).

These verses tell us that if we are intimate with the Lord, and faithful to Him and all that is His, He will speak to us clearly.

Jesus also said a similar thing to His disciples when they asked why He spoke to the people in parables:

Because the knowledge of the secrets of the kingdom of heaven is given to you, but not to them. For whoever has, more shall be given, and he will have an abundance. But whoever does not have, even what he has shall be taken away from him. Therefore I speak to them in parables… (Matthew 13:11-12 NIV).

Jesus often spoke in parables to the crowds, and then explained the meanings privately to his disciples. Jesus was saying that because they desired to be close to Him, He could speak plainly to them. They had more than the crowds did—they had intimacy and love for Jesus— so He gave them more than others. In this case, that "more" was plain language rather than figurative.

As we discussed, Jesus also explained that He spoke in parables so those with hardened hearts wouldn't be able to understand what He meant (Mathew 13:15).

When we are close to the Lord, like Moses and the disciples, we have the extreme honor, at times, to hear Him clearly, "face-to-face." At other times, our hearts are calloused about an issue (though not totally hardened against the Lord) and He must speak to us in symbols or parables, so we will seek Him for the interpretation and get our hearts clear.

Riddles

At times, we can have a dream that has no mental picture and is simply the voice of the Lord or an angel, but instead of clear direction, instruction, or warning, He speaks in a riddle, puzzle, or some other quizzical phrase or statement. Treat these dreams like other symbolic dreams, meaning something is wrong and needs some kind of correction. There is an example of a riddle in Chapter Two.

Foretelling Dreams/ Dreams with Numbers

Most dreams don't have specific numbers in them, but when they do, they could be an indicator of future events. In Scripture, many of the dreams that were of a foretelling pattern had exact numbers in them.

When I use the term *numbers* I mean exact numbers, not such things as, "There were a few mean dogs in the dream; I think maybe four;" instead, "There were exactly four mean dogs." The numbers in a dream that can be foretelling are those that stand out specifically in the dreamer's recollection.

Even with Foretelling Dreams/Dreams with Numbers, it indicates a correction of some kind if the dreams are in symbolic form rather than a clear voice of the Lord or an angel.

For example, let's talk about the other Joseph, the one we commonly think of when we talk about dreams. The Lord used a dream to foretell his future, while at the same time brought correction to him.

Joseph's Dreams Were Foretelling and Brought Correction

Life's circumstances that occur at the time of your dreams, as well as those in Scripture, are important factors to know in order to find the correct interpretation. In the Scriptural account of Genesis 37:1-10, Jacob favored his seventeen-year-old son Joseph and gave him a beautiful coat, which exacerbated his brothers' hatred toward him. Favoritism can cause a child to be not only the object of his parents' affection, but narcissistic and disliked by their siblings.

Jacob, Joseph's father, also had brother issues and for the same reasons—Jacob's mother favored him over his brother Esau. Manipulation of parents and siblings by the favored child was a generational issue in his family. The meaning of the name Jacob is *deceiver*, and that is what he was the first part of his life. He then went through a fourteen-year process until his flesh was subdued, so that his spirit could submit to the Lord's ways. At that point, the Lord changed his name to Israel, meaning *one who prevails with God*. Jacob struggled with being the favored child when young, and his son Joseph had the same issue.

Joseph's special coat made his brothers jealous; they hated him so much they couldn't even speak nicely to him. During this time, Joseph had been out in the field feeding the flock with his brothers, and ran home and told on them to Dad. Likely his intention was to get them into trouble. No doubt the tension and bitter treatment from his brothers (although possibly deserved) was on his mind a lot. So, he had a dream and told it to his brothers.

Joseph's dreams did indicate future events, but they also brought correction—for himself.

> He [Joseph] said to them, "Listen to this dream I had: We were binding sheaves of grain out in the field when suddenly my sheaf rose and stood upright, while your sheaves gathered around mine and bowed down to it" (Genesis 37:7 NIV).

This dream uses grain as a symbol, and grain would be the issue in years to come. The fact that Joseph's sheaf stood upright while the brothers' bowed down to it indicates leadership for Joseph but servitude for the brothers. They hated him even more for telling them this dream.

His brothers said to him, "Do you intend to reign over us? Will you actually rule us?" And they hated him all the more because of his dream and what he had said (Genesis 37:8 NIV).

This dream contained symbols, which needed interpretation. It wasn't a clear, specific voice of instruction. Remember, the Lord spoke directly to Joseph, Mary's husband, with clear instruction. He could have spoken directly to Joseph and said, "When you're older, you will provide food for your family." But He didn't; the dream had symbols, which are meant to bring conviction, correction, instruction, and discipline, as we discussed in Chapter Four.

Two Similar Dreams in a Close Timeline Can Be Foretelling

Joseph had another dream, and it also was symbolic and needed interpretation; however, this one contained numbers. He told this one to his brothers and father, as he had the first one.

"Listen," he said, "I had another dream, and this time the sun and moon and eleven stars were bowing down to me" (Genesis 37:9 NIV).

Since this was his second very similar dream in a short period, it indicated a foretelling set of dreams. According to Genesis 41:32, when you have two dreams with the same meaning, in a short timeline, it is established the Lord will cause it to happen, and soon. However, for Joseph, "soon" would mean thirteen years, much like the fourteen years it took for his father to overcome his deceiving ways in order to fulfill the Lord's purposes.

A second indicator of the foretelling pattern for this dream is the appearance of a specific number—eleven. Specific numbers can indicate time in dreams, but you must consider the dream in its entirety to know for sure.

Fox example, seven cows and seven stalks of grain were representative for seven years in Pharaoh's dreams in Genesis Chapter 41; the cupbearer's three vines and baker's three baskets in Chapter 40 each indicated three days.

Using specific numbers to establish whether a dream has foretelling aspects is a guideline rather than a rule. It certainly seems the eleven stars were symbolic for his eleven brothers while the sun and moon symbolized his parents, and these numbers total thirteen. It was thirteen years from the time of his dreams until he was set into a leadership role. It's possible the numbers could represent time in this dream.

Joseph's second dream, like the first one, was in symbols, which indicates a need for correction. This dream showed his whole universe bowing down to him, and his father rebuked him, saying, "Are your mother, brothers, and I to bow ourselves to the earth to you?" He seemed to see pride in Joseph's heart because of the dreams, rather than being excited his favorite son could be elevated to leadership. Jacob was concerned about his son's dreams.

Both of Joseph's dreams were meant to bring a combination of correction of his pride (Job 33/Symbolic dreams) and foretelling (Foretelling Dreams/Dreams with Numbers). This can sometimes be true when dreams contain symbols and specific numbers.

Since Joseph had two similar dreams with a parallel meaning in a short period, it was an indicator of foretelling, according to Genesis 41:32. God's intention was to correct Joseph's issues so that he could be used for God's purposes foretold in the dreams.

In contrast to Joseph's dreams, Solomon was also a young man called to a great destiny and leadership role. He burned a thousand sacrifices to show his love for the Lord and that night had a dream in which the Lord appeared to him. As Solomon slept, the Lord said, *"Ask what I shall give to you." (1 Kings 3:5)* Solomon's answer showed humility, and for this, the Lord commended him. His dream was the clear voice of the Lord with no mental picture; therefore, there were no symbols to interpret and no correction implied.

Joseph's dreams were different. They weren't a clear voice of the Lord; therefore, they weren't meant to bring clear warning or instruction. Both of his dreams were like Job 33/Symbolic dreams, so they contained an element of correction.

Even though his dreams seem to call him to a place of leadership, consider the way God calls one to a position of authority. True leadership is a call to service and humility, not to arrogance. This dream is incorrectly interpreted, "You will rule over your family; they will bow down to you." Joseph was called to be a forgiving, loving servant to his family in years to come, when the condition of his heart changed. His dreams were calling him, but they were pointing out his heart issues that had to be dealt with first.

As we will see later with Nebuchadnezzar's first dream, Joseph's dreams also seem to say "he is the greatest," but the dreams were meant to convict him of prideful attitudes. The appearance of symbols in a dream indicates a need for some kind of correction.

Whether speaking directly to you, through a prophetic word, or in a dream, when the Lord speaks a word for your future, you must be changed and conformed until you fit the purposes of the word.

Looking at the story of the cupbearer and baker's dreams in Genesis Chapter 40, Pharaoh's former servants were in prison when each had a dream containing specific numbers, and their dreams came to pass. Both their dreams were in symbols, which showed a need for conviction or some kind of correction in their thinking or mindset.

In addition, their dreams were similar and occurred the same night, and in the same location, even though to two different people, which is a possibility to consider as a foretelling element.

Pharaoh's Dreams: Foretelling and Direction

Pharaoh had two similar dreams in one night, which indicated that the point the dreams addressed was established by God and would come to pass soon. His dreams were symbolic and needed interpretation, so they contained a form of conviction or correction in his thinking or mindset. Before the dreams, perhaps Pharaoh had no intention to ration and save a portion of grain, and there was nothing in the storehouses.

Not All Dreams with Specific Numbers Are Foretelling

At times, there will be dreams with numbers in them that aren't of the foretelling pattern.

Sandi, a young pastor's wife, called me early one morning with a dream that seemed to be foretelling because of the specific numbers in it. Sandi said, "I saw the exact number, as well as the appearance of angels, and thought the dream must be foretelling."

"I dreamed there was a group of troubled teens and we were trying to help them. In the background was a big city and something exploded. I could see there was substantial damage.

The scene changed: Angels were writing numbers in the sky. I can only remember one of the numbers—10. A couple of angels were on the ground. It seemed the angels were dressed in white, but as I looked closer, I realized they were dressed in dark clothes. I was concerned about the explosion."

As she told me the dream, I heard a Job 33/Symbolic pattern emerge, even though there were angels and a specific number. The first clue was the angels were "dream angels" rather than a real angel speaking a clear message in the dream, and second, the negative symbolism of their dark clothing that had previously appeared light. I asked Sandi about what had happened in her life the day before, particularly if there was an "explosion" between people.

"My husband and I were angry with one another, and yes, there was an 'explosion' between us," she said. "My first thoughts when I had this dream were about end-times and God's judgment." (Often our first thoughts about the dream's meaning aren't the intended interpretation, but an emotional or logical reaction.)

"Now that I think about the argument we had last night, I thought I was taking a stand for a godly position. However, the white clothes, that at first seemed to represent holy angels, were actually dark clothes when I looked closer. I think this means my message and delivery were coming from a wrong place."

The number ten means a trial or time of testing and the argument between Sandi and her husband was definitely trying for them.

Remember to look at all symbols in a dream and consider any heart issues first, in case the dreams are meant to bring correction that we might be healed and/or set on the right path.

Mixed Pattern of Symbols and Foretelling Without Numbers

Nebuchadnezzar's dreams indicate the future in ways other than the presence of specific numbers. Both his dreams were supernaturally interpreted and were given for correction and foretelling. You can read the story of the king's dreams in Daniel Chapter Two.

Nebuchadnezzar's dreams contain a treasure chest of knowledge about how many dreams work.

The king dreamed the first dream and it greatly troubled him, even though he couldn't remember it when he awoke. As Daniel slept the next night, the Lord gave him a dream, and in it, He showed him the king's dream and its interpretation. In his dream, Daniel saw

Nebuchadnezzar lying in bed wondering about end times before he fell asleep. The Lord gave the king an answer about that very thing, the same night, in a dream.

The Lord gives keys and insights into secrets as we sleep. Sometimes He talks about what's on His mind, but usually He addresses the topics we are pondering. This is an important clue to interpretation.

Nebuchadnezzar's first dream was of an enormous, dazzlingly beautiful statue with a head of gold, chest and arms made of silver, belly and thighs of bronze, legs of iron, and feet of partly iron and partly clay.

While the king was watching in the dream, a supernatural rock struck the statue and smashed its feet, and then the iron, clay, bronze, silver, and gold were all broken into pieces and blown completely away by the wind. The rock then became a huge mountain and filled the whole earth.

Daniel told the interpretation that was given to him in his dream, saying the head of gold represented the king and his kingdom; God had given Nebuchadnezzar authority over all mankind and animals. He said more kingdoms would be built in the future by men, then the Lord would cause the kingdoms of the world to become His own (Revelation 11:15).

Daniel knew this was a foretelling dream because the Lord gave him both the dream and its interpretation as he slept.

The king's dream contained implied correction: Nebuchadnezzar and others to come, throughout the ages, would build worldly empires, and eventually God would strike down all man-made kingdoms and establish His own.

God had given Nebuchadnezzar the entire known world to lead, but he was full of pride. At first glance, the king's dream, like those of Joseph, seems to indicate God saying, "The king is the greatest." That wasn't God's point in the dream. In reality, Nebuchadnezzar saw himself as a god and didn't credit the Lord for putting him in the position of leadership. He was building his own kingdom, as would those after him.

In this dream, like those of Joseph, we see an important dream principle: some dreams mess with our pride. Sometimes our pride grows stronger because of the dream. This dream wasn't intended to build the king's pride, it was meant to correct it. The application of the dream was for him to repent and give all credit to God.

It's easy to interpret a dream in an opposite way of the Lord's intention when we don't know His purposes in giving dreams.

The king was represented as the head of gold in the large statue. His pride caused him to respond to the dream by erecting a giant golden statue to his own image, like the golden head of the statue in his dream, and commanding the entire nation to worship him. The dream from God was the catalyst the enemy used to enlarge the king's pride.

Like the king, most of us want to believe all prophetic revelation is building us up, not correcting us. Learning the difference, being teachable, and asking for humility will take us on a quicker road to a pure heart and spiritual maturity. All our lives we are in a process of being conformed to the image of Jesus. Dreams are one of many tools He uses to accomplish this transformation.

Daniel said God had given the king authority over all mankind and animals. This is important; remember these words. They show up in the king's next dream.

Nebuchadnezzar's Second Dream

When telling Daniel his second dream, the king described himself as content and prosperous. Oblivious of the pride in his heart, he felt all was right in his world and couldn't imagine why he would have a bad dream. God's intention in giving him the second dream was similar to the first, but it contained a clear reprimand and foretold judgment because of his pride.

Nebuchadnezzar said the second dream terrified him, but the Bible tells us it was from the Lord, not the enemy. In it, he saw an enormous tree, full of fruit and food for all mankind and animals, and visible to all the earth.

Then he saw an angel from Heaven cry out for the tree (we are told later in the story the tree was symbolic for the king) to be cut down, while leaving its stump and roots in the ground, and for him to have the mind of an animal and live like one for seven years.

The angel said that God had made the verdict so all people would know the Lord is sovereign over every kingdom, and that He sets them up and tears them down as He wishes.

Now we can see the common thread between the two dreams. When interpreting the first dream, Daniel said that God had given the king authority over all mankind and animals. The king's second dream began with a huge tree that fed all mankind and animals. These symbols show up in the second dream to give the dreamer—the king—a clue that this dream was a continuum, in some ways, of the first. In the first dream, there was implied correction for the king's pride but his reaction was to build a statue and have all people worship him or die. The second dream is a warning of impending judgment, because he didn't heed the correction of the first dream and repent. The consequence of not heeding the Lord's correction, just like the results described in Job 33, was insanity, a sickness for sure.

Daniel was greatly perplexed and terrified to interpret the dream. He explained that the tree was symbolic for the king, who had responsibility over a great part of the known world at that time.

He explained that the Lord had issued a decree for the king to be driven away from people and live like a madman, a wild animal, for seven years. The symbol of the stump left in the ground (potential for future growth and restoration) meant the king would have an opportunity to repent after that time and be restored to his position.

Daniel begged the king to repent immediately in order to avoid the consequences, but the king didn't heed Daniel's admonishment to repent. One year later it happened just as the angel had said, and he lost his mind and lived as an animal. The king came to his right mind after seven years in the wild and repented for his pride and actions. He was restored to his position, and declared God to be sovereign over all.

The first part of the second dream was given in symbols, and was correction. In the middle portion an angel appeared, speaking clear warning of future events for the king.

The end of the dream, like the first part, was in symbols because time would tell if the king would heed the warning, receive conviction, and repent.

When you have a dream that has a part in which you hear the clear voice of the Lord or an angel (which most likely means foretelling), and a totally different part that is given in symbols (which mean there is something that you must either correct, or there is something yet unclear to you that must be revealed), you must interpret the symbolic portion and make any necessary adjustments in order for the clear, foretelling portion to come to pass.

Should the symbols indicate judgment, like Nebuchadnezzar's second dream, you must repent to avoid the consequences foretold in the dream.

Dreams for Others

Usually dreams are all about you. Although the star character in a dream could be another person, that person is usually symbolic for a part of you. They represent a trait or situation you have in common with that person's past or present experience at the time of the dream.

For example, let's say you have a friend named Candy who is easily intimidated, and one day you are in a difficult situation in which you allow a controlling person to bully you. Then that night you dream of your friend Candy. Most likely, your friend will represent the part of you that was intimidated in the difficult situation the day before.

In that case, the Lord would be bringing your weakness to the forefront for you to learn how to better handle such situations and forgive the bully. Here's another example: Maybe your cousin was spoiled terribly as a child, and she appeared in your dream last night. She could represent a part of you that acted or reacted in a self-centered way about a situation the day before the dream. Should this scenario occur, the Lord would give you the dream because He wants to you face it, repent, and mature in that area of your life.

Those dreams in which a person is not representing a part of you, but the dream is for the benefit of that person, are rare. You should always consider a person in a dream to symbolize a part of you, unless you truly can't make it work after praying and meditating on it for a time. Still then, always remember you could still be wrong about your interpretation, especially if the dream seems to cast the person in a negative light. As we covered previously, the Lord doesn't gossip.

Please be careful telling dreams to others that you consider are for them or for other people. Don't start a wildfire, based on a dream that could be misinterpreted, that could hurt people.

We can beat people up with a wrong interpretation of dreams. I can't be clear enough on this point.

While greeting others in a Sunday morning service, a woman standing beside me spoke to a man who came to say hello to her family. "You wouldn't believe what your wife did in my dream last night!" she exclaimed. The poor man's big Sunday-morning smile fell like a concrete block as fear and embarrassment hit him. It was obvious he thought the dream could have revealed something terrible about his wife to this prophetic person and to everyone around who heard her statement.

Far too often, people say they have been "warned" about another person through a dream and consequently severed relationship with them. Symbolic dreams aren't for the purpose of warning, they are correction for the dreamer.

From Genesis through Revelation, the Bible is a story of God's love for each of us and of His great desire for us to love Him first, and then one another, as much as we love ourselves. Jesus said we are to forgive one another endless times and He spoke often of his desire for us to be in unity.

Only in extremely rare instances does He reveal the sins or shortcomings of another through prophetic venues, including dreams. Of all the dreams I've heard, there have only been two in which the Lord revealed the issues of another person, and in both instances, it was a dear family member of the dreamer. On both occasions, the Lord gave the dream so the dreamer would know how to pray and how to handle a relationship in a more productive way with the beloved family member.

For Him to give a dream to create disunity would be against His Word. He isn't a gossip. He loves all people. He isn't an accuser. The devil is that.

It should be re-emphasized that dreams for the benefit of another person are rare; the total numbers of them are far less than one percent of all dreams. However, on the rare occasion that one person's dream is for another, it is to be viewed more as prophecy than a dream.

1 Corinthians 14:3 states the reasons for prophecy: to build a person up (edification), to stir them up (exhortation), and to comfort them. Don't allow the enemy to tell you that exhortation contains a license for you to tear others down with prophetic revelation.

He will never give you a dream for someone with whom you are offended, angry, or have any other negative emotion. He only gives dreams with a message for another when the two of you are in a healthy relationship and you have been interceding for that person with a heart of love.

Having made that clear, He does give us dreams at rare times for another for whom we have been interceding or whom we love. If you believe the Lord is showing you negative things about another person or ministry, you become responsible—to the Lord—for how you handle that situation.

Many church leaders have given their lives to serve the Lord and have been bitten by the sheep. If you truly believe you have been given a dream for leadership, bear in mind the amount of misinterpreted, accusatory dreams pastors and ministries receive. Pray, pray, pray for understanding and for the right time and person with whom to share the dream. Wild, accusatory fires, based on lies, have spread and hurt many because of misinterpreted dreams.

Here's one of the few I've had that was for someone else:

I dreamed I saw a minister I knew and there were two of her standing side-by-side. One looked just like her and the other was a bigger, depressed, unhealthy-looking version of her. The two versions were looking at one another.

The scene changed and I saw a huge arena full of people who were waiting and cheering for her to come onto the scene.

When I awoke, I tried to make the dream about me. I prayed and thought of ways she could symbolize a part of me, and anything in the dream that could pertain to my thoughts, motives, or actions the day or two before. At that time, I had never seen a symbolic dream for someone else. Finally I thought, *My gosh, it looks like this is actually for this minister, that she is depressed and unhealthy. Could the Lord be saying I should call and tell her about the dream, and that there is an arena full of people who need her?*

I was afraid to call her. I didn't know her well, but she spoke at my church often and I thought highly of her teaching gift. However, it seemed like there was a slight tugging on me to call her. *No way*, I thought, fell back asleep and dreamed again:

I was wearing yellow flip-flops. Then I heard a voice, "You could have at least put it out for usury."

I awoke with a start. Usury! That's what the Lord said to the wicked servant when he failed to use the talents he had been given. Flip-flops symbolized I was "flip-flopping" over the decision of whether to obey what seemed to be the Lord. Yellow symbolized my fear of calling her.

Immediately upon interpreting the dream, I did call, and gave her a jillion disclaimers, asking for her grace in case I was wrong. Finally she interrupted me, "Please just tell me what happened in the dream. I'm desperate. You have no idea what I'm going through."

It meant so much to her that the Lord had given me a dream for her benefit. Like with prophecy, the Lord was giving encouragement for her. The fact the dream was in symbols indicated correction was needed, but it was loving, kind correction to call her to a higher place—for her to cast aside the depression that was holding her back and realize she was still needed in ministry. The Lord's word of encouragement had the power in it to pull her up to overcome the negative events in her life at that time.

Key Points in This Chapter:

- Dreams with no mental picture but a clear voice of the Lord or an angel tend to be foretelling, bring warning, or give instruction, and they should be interpreted literally.

- Many times after pondering a topic then falling asleep, a dream addresses that topic. This occurs regardless of the pattern into which the dream falls.

- When we are intimate with Him, the Lord sometimes speaks to us clearly rather than in symbols, riddles, or parables.

- Most dreams don't have specific numbers in them, but when they do, they could be an indicator of future events.

- Joseph's dreams were foretelling and also brought correction.

- Two similar dreams occurring within a close timeline can be foretelling.

- Not all dreams with specific numbers are foretelling.

- It's always best to look first at events that happened the day before the dream, and our attitudes about them, when interpreting a dream.

- Nebuchadnezzar's dreams were foretelling and also brought correction.

- Usually dreams are all about you. Although the star character or a minor role in a dream could be another person, that person is usually symbolic for a part of you.

- The Lord gives encouragement, exhortation, and comfort in dreams that are truly for other people.

CHAPTER NINE

Interpreting Dreams
As a Ministry

Some of you are called to ministry. You often hear the dreams of others and try to help them solve their puzzles. This group includes pastors, counselors, and those with inner-healing/deliverance ministries, among others. The Lord also uses those who have wisdom and other spiritual gifts to help solve dream puzzles for others, including angels that speak a message from the Lord.

Proper interpretation of dreams is a powerful spiritual tool to help others see issues that hinder their healing or keep them distant from the Lord. Job 33:24 tells us that God extends grace to those who know someone to interpret their dreams.

Even though the Church, and the world for that matter, has a great need for proper dream interpretation, there are those in ministry who have been burned by the dreams of others and are now wary of the topic as a whole. Others in leadership are tempted to discount dreams but continue to try to hear the Lord through them.

Tom, the head of a worldwide missions group, recently told me a story about a misinterpreted dream that caused devastating consequences for a good friend of his, Doug.

Doug was a Christian businessman who worked in management at a large, highly successful company owned by a Christian family. Practically everyone in the office was a strong believer and attended the church where Doug was in leadership.

Someone in the office dreamed that Doug was having an affair with his secretary. The dreamer told the dream to some co-workers, who then began having dreams of their own about Doug and his secretary.

Even though innocent of any wrongdoing, in order to protect his reputation, he fired the secretary, a godly young woman and devout member of the church.

The consequences of the misinterpretation were severe for numerous people, but devastating for the secretary, and it sent her into a tailspin. She couldn't believe these nice people from church had believed a lie that resulted in losing her job and making her appear to be involved in an adulterous affair with her boss. Getting fired made it look as though she was guilty of wrongdoing. Brokenhearted and confused, she turned her back on her church and the Lord.

All of this chaos started with a misinterpreted dream.

When Tom told me the situation, I explained that the dream, like all Job 33/Symbolic dreams, was for and about the dreamer. From much experience interpreting dreams of this pattern, I surmised a likely scenario that had prompted Doug's appearance in the co-worker's dream. I figured it was possible that Doug had an issue in the past with a woman outside of his marriage, and it was known by the dreamer and some others at work. So, in the dream, Doug was likely representing the dreamer, who was currently having an affair of some kind, whether mental, emotional, or physical, and likely with a woman at work. Apparently, the dreamer's heart was calloused about his own sin, and he was blind to the correlation the Holy Spirit was using by having Doug appear as a symbolic character in the dream.

Tom laughed and said, "That's very close to the truth of what happened!"

But not understanding how dreams work, no one in leadership knew what to do at the time. Leadership had believed Doug to be innocent of accusations made by the co-worker, but they had no idea what the dream meant. They knew he had made a mistake and over-reacted when he fired the secretary, who was the biggest victim in this instance of bad dream interpretation.

Like Nebuchadnezzar and his dream of the head of gold, we jump to conclusions and take the dream's meaning opposite to the Lord's intention. It's extremely important that we don't come to quick conclusions about a dream's meaning that seem to address another person's sin, but rather take time, pray, and look at all symbols and aspects of the dream. It's important to remember God is not a gossip, and doesn't tell a person's secrets or sins to others. It's also important to remember that people in our dreams are symbolic for parts of us.

Rather than the interpretation leading the dreamer closer to Jesus, all this misinterpreted bad fruit made a mockery of dreams and hurt many people, especially the young, innocent secretary.

Again, this dream was for the dreamer and his correction, but wrong interpretation led others to believe wrong ideas.

My prayer is for the spirits of Truth and Revelation to surround dream interpretation, and for the Church to begin to embrace the Lord's intentions to convict and correct us through most of them.

There is a direct correlation between the Lord pouring out dreams in the end-times and making his Bride spotless, without sin. The purpose of dreams is to clean us up and draw us closer to the Lord.

It's All about Jesus

Knowing the Lord's voice and obeying Him when He speaks are two of the most important elements in our lives. We have given our lives and declared Him our Savior and Lord.

Our highest calling is to know Him and His voice, in every way He speaks, whether Scripture, dreams, visions, prophecy, signs, wonders, whispers, tugs on our heart, or an audible voice. We don't want to miss an important point the Lord is making.

The number one job of a minister is to direct others to Jesus. Like all else, dreams exist for Jesus and the Cross. At the root of each dream is His intention for us to be saved, healed, and delivered, and to live the life for which He paid.

He came to do the ministry proclaimed in Isaiah 61: to save, heal every aspect of your life, deliver you from bondage, and bring favor. He also came to destroy the devil's work of stealing, killing, and destruction, according to Luke 10. The Lord still ministers for all those same reasons in dreams.

He is sending you to others to do those exact things. If you will focus on these works Jesus came to do, you will see He still does the same in all revelation, including dreams.

A Right Heart

Years ago when I first began interpreting dreams, I had some understanding of dream interpretation but little wisdom. I met with one young lady whose dreams showed she was having an affair. Without thinking, I bluntly told her what I saw in her dream, without considering her feelings or possible embarrassment. *After all*, I reasoned, *if God didn't want me to tell her, then why did He give me this understanding and send her to me?*

That night, I had a dream in which I had people lined up and shot them, then another where I killed everyone and put them into the freezer with arms and legs sticking out randomly. It sounds funny (and a little grotesque) now, since dreams are often ridiculous in presentation, but it wasn't funny at the time.

When I realized I was "killing" people with the frankness of my words, I asked Him to give me compassion and grace for those who came to me with dreams. I learned to speak a disclaimer to bypass the person's strong mindsets and any shame the enemy might throw at them.

One way I do that is to tell them briefly about my own failures in areas similar to theirs. That's not always easy to do, yet it does tend to set people, especially if they don't know you well, more at ease when they know they're not being judged. It's important to minister to people from a kind heart and to keep our heart free from judgments and criticism. We are here to facilitate healing.

Being transparent isn't easy for many people. It's uncomfortable to tell your sins and weaknesses to another person. It isn't always easy to be open and transparent with the Lord, either. After all, isn't that why Adam and Eve hid from God in the garden?

As interpreters, counselors, and ministers, our job is to be softhearted and kind, knowing He is allowing us a view into people's hearts and wounds, and wants to do a deep work in them. Like a doctor or nurse, a kind bedside manner can be as important as talent and skill, while the Lord does surgery on hearts right in front of us.

When the Lord uses you to interpret the dreams of others, you must take great care to never discuss their secrets with others. If you are in a position to help a child of the King, neither He nor they will appreciate your indiscretion.

Melissa, a middle-aged banker and her husband Ronnie, a successful salesman, were in the midst of a divorce because of his physical and emotional abuse. During this time, Ronnie met with one of the young pastors at their church and was able to convince him to believe his side of the story, which didn't include the truth about his abusive behavior. The young pastor took Ronnie's side, and when he finally met with Melissa, he blamed her for the issues and refused to listen to her side of the story. The added pain of rejection and betrayal from her church convinced her to never again expose her pain to leadership again.

Some years later, she was still hesitant to expose herself to anyone and kept herself guarded. One day, she had lunch with a new friend from church who had just ministered with an inner-healing group to a woman with significant issues. To Melissa's shock, the friend openly discussed the woman's issues from the ministry session, even to the point of saying her name and discussing "what a mess" the woman was. For many years, these experiences kept Melissa from trusting anyone to help her find healing for her own wounds.

This is not the way of love, nor the way of the Lord. If we are called to ministry, first of all, we are called to love. We are to be "safe" for others.

The Royal Law of Love

> *If you really keep the royal law found in Scripture, "Love your neighbor as yourself," you are doing right (James 2:8 NIV).*

This commandment calls us up to the highest standard, the one of a King, and royal dignity toward other people.

If we are called to ministry, which in its essence means helping others get closer to Jesus, our ministry won't have abundant anointing or fruit unless we have compassion. Jesus healed people because of His compassion, His love, and His sympathetic heart for their pain and suffering. In order to have compassion, we must have love.

Consider the following traits of love from 1 Corinthians 13 as a prerequisite for our hearts before we minister to others about their pain, shame, sin, addictions, and more.

Love is patient and kind. Love is not jealous or boastful or proud or rude. It does not demand its own way. It is not irritable, and it keeps no record of being wronged. It does not rejoice about injustice but rejoices whenever the truth wins out. Love never gives up, never loses faith, is always hopeful, and endures through every circumstance (1 Corinthians 13:4-7 NLT).

If you fail in any of the above aspects of love—and we all do—you can repent and ask the Lord to teach you how to love. He wants to use you to minister to others, and to be a servant. The Lord calls us to a life of servitude. We minister to people because of our love for Him and His great love for people.

If you make a mistake, admit it and move on. God gives grace to the humble.

The Process

Solving dream puzzles takes time. It's a ministry, an art, truly a learned skill. It takes time, patience, humility, and love, in both the dreamer and interpreter, to arrive at the correct interpretation.

The process of interpreting dreams for others is much the same as interpreting one of your own. Let's take another quick look at that process:

- Write the dream as the dreamer tells you.

- Underline the symbols.

- Write what they feel the symbols could represent. Use the Symbol Dictionary or Chapter Five in this book as a guide to help find the meanings for symbols.

- Pray with the dreamer and ask the Holy Spirit to open their heart and guide you both to the truth about the situation that the dream addresses. Ask Him to remind the dreamer of what happened the day or two before the dream that was trouble-some, and to help you both think in figurative language.

- Look for a thread: Focus on people the dreamer knows in the dream, then on colors and places.

- Ask questions. Lots of them, giving the dreamer time to an-swer. Listen well to their answers. They will likely tell you a story of an event that happened in the previous couple of days that has been bothering them, and you will see the thread begin to appear and the dream's meaning unravel.

- Look for an "Ah-ha! Moment" when suddenly they "feel" the interpretation is correct. I've found the Holy Spirit usually works this way—you can suddenly sense they are connecting with the true issue that He is bringing up in the dream. Until they do, something is likely a little "off" in the interpretation, unless they are guarding themselves and refusing to expose their weaknesses.

Some dreamers aren't able to answer your questions because they don't want to expose their flaws. Some feel they would be gossip-ing if they were to tell you bad things about a person that appeared in the dream as a symbol. Reassure them you will be a safe place for them (and do so) and that the Lord wants a particular issue with which they are struggling to be healed and set free through the dream. You can't push them, however. You can only explain and give them the oppor-tunity to be transparent. Some people aren't ready, although most are.

Help Them Apply Interpretation

Once you and the dreamer have arrived at the correct interpretation, you should try to help them find the best application. Should they repent? Need deliverance? Change their point-of-view, direction? Some of all the above? Gently guide them toward the Lord and His ministry of healing, deliverance, and encouragement. You can pray with them, or leave them to pray alone if they are uncomfortable, though leave them with guidelines for prayer if they need them.

Key Points in This Chapter:

- The number one job of a minister is to direct others to Jesus.

- When interpreting dreams for others, speak kind words to make them feel at ease. Transparency and vulnerability aren't easy for some people.

- If we are called to ministry, which in its essence means helping others get closer to Jesus, our ministry won't have abundant anointing or fruit unless we have compassion.

- The process of helping others interpret a dream is similar to interpreting your own:

    1. Write the dream as the dreamer tells you.

    2. Underline the symbols.

    3. Write what they feel the symbols could represent. Use the Symbol Dictionary or Chapter Five in this book as a guide to help find the meanings for symbols.

    4. Pray with the dreamer and ask the Holy Spirit to open their heart and guide you both to the truth about the situation that the dream addresses. Ask Him to remind the dreamer of what happened the day or two before the dream that was troublesome, and to help you both think in figurative language.

    5. Look for a thread.

    6. Focus on people the dreamer knows in the dream, then on colors and places.

7. Ask questions, lots of them, giving the dreamer time to answer. Listen well to their answers.

8. Look for an "Ah-ha! Moment" when suddenly they "feel" the interpretation is correct.

9. Help the dreamer apply the correct interpretation to their life.

Symbol Dictionary

This symbol dictionary is not a comprehensive one. You will have dreams containing symbols that aren't included here and will need to know how to find meanings for them. Please read Chapter Five for more in-depth information to help you find meanings for symbols.

In this dictionary, you'll find Numbers and Colors are separated from Miscellaneous, meaning all other symbols. I have included more detailed explanations for the Numbers and Colors using the Principle of First Mention (see Chapter Five), to show you how to derive the meanings of symbols. You can then use the symbols in these two sections as examples to understand how figurative language works, and how their meanings correlate to Scripture.

In the Miscellaneous section, you'll find some explanation at times, but for many symbols, I've only provided their possible meanings. Many of the terms in this section are mentioned in Scripture, and you can look those up in a concordance. Some I determined through dictionaries; the Lord spoke some of them to others or me as we slept. All symbols in this dictionary have been used helping dreamers interpret their dreams.

Figurative Language

Understanding how the Lord uses symbolism, one type of figurative language, is a requirement to understand dream interpretation. As I mentioned earlier, dream interpretation is an art, not a science. You must apply yourself and learn to think in figurative language.

You'll find that sometimes the storyline, as well as the symbols, is also given in figurative language.

Positive or Negative

Many symbols can have either a positive or a negative meaning, depending on the use in the dream. You'll notice many of the symbols in this dictionary have both positive and negative possibilities, and at times you must consider the entire dream to determine a symbol's correct application. A common mistake is to always assume every symbol is positive—remember the Lord is often working in our hearts and exposing those things that keep us from Him, so don't disregard that He could be showing you something "negative" that He wants to heal.

NUMBERS

One: First; beginning; light; revelation; understanding

> *God said, "Let there be light and there was light"… the first day (Genesis 1:3-5 KJV).*

Two: Divide; separate; separate the holy from the unholy

> *God said, "Let there be a firmament in the midst of the waters and let it divide the waters from the waters"… the second day Genesis 1:6-8 KJV).*

Three: Be the same as others; copy; reproduce

> *God said, "Let the earth bring forth grass, the herb yielding seed and the fruit tree yielding fruit after his kind, whose seed is in itself"… the third day (Genesis 1:11-13 KJV).*

Four: Rule; reign; mentor; leadership

> *God made two great lights; the greater light to rule the day and the lesser light to rule the night…the fourth day (Genesis 1:16-19 KJV).*

Five: Multiply; abundance; fruitful

> *God said, "Let the waters bring forth abundantly the moving creature that has life, and fowl that may fly above the earth"…and God blessed them saying, "Be fruitful and multiply"…the fifth day (Genesis 1:20-23 KJV).*

Six: Mankind; image; carnality; God's love for man

> *God said, Let us make man in our image, after our likeness…the sixth day Genesis 1:26-31 KJV).*

Seven: A complete cycle; rest; finish; God's perfect rest; ceasing from labor

> *The heavens and earth were finished... on the seventh day God ended his work... he rested on the seventh day (Genesis 2:1-3 KJV).*

The numbers eight through ten are found in other parts of Scripture rather than the first two chapters of Genesis.

Eight: Seven means a complete cycle; therefore, eight is a new beginning.

> *For the generations to come every male among you who is eight days old must be circumcised... (Genesis 17:12 NIV).*

Nine: Harvest; fruition

> *While you plant during the eighth year, you will eat from the old crop and will continue to eat from it until the harvest of the ninth year comes in (Leviticus 25:22 NIV).*

Ten: A trial or testing

> *The waters continued to recede until the tenth month, and on the first day of the tenth month the tops of the mountains became visible (Genesis 8:5 NIV).*

The numbers eleven through nineteen, generally speaking, are opposites of one through nine.

Eleven: Finished; almost finished, practically the end of a cycle, you're almost there. Example: When there were only eleven apostles, they appointed a twelfth so the number would be complete.

Twelve: Bringing together for a common purpose; family; government. Examples: Jacob had twelve sons; there were twelve tribes, twelve disciples, and twelve apostles.

Thirteen: Rebellion; being forced to serve; cutting off the old. Example: Ishmael was thirteen when he was circumcised.

> *For twelve years they had been subject to Kedorlaomer, but in the thirteenth year they rebelled (Genesis 14:3-5 NIV).*

Fourteen: Bondage; double

> *It was like this for the twenty years I was in your household. I worked for you fourteen years for your two daughters and six years for your flocks, and you changed my wages ten times (Genesis 31:41 NIV).*

Fifteen: Sin covered; grace; evil stopped

> *The waters rose and covered the mountains to a depth of more than fifteen cubits. Every living thing that moved on land perished—birds, livestock, wild animals, all the creatures that swarm over the earth, and all mankind (Genesis 7:20-21 NIV).*

Sixteen: Limitless; without boundaries

> *These were the children born to Jacob by Zilpah, whom Laban had given to his daughter Leah—sixteen in all (Genesis 46:18 NIV).*

Seventeen: Incomplete; transition

> *And the ark rested in the seventh month, the seventeenth day of the month, on the mountains of Ararat (Genesis 8:4 KJV).*

Eighteen: An ending; death; oppression

> *For eighteen years they oppressed all the Israelites east of the Jordan River in the land of the Amorites (Judges 10:8 NIV).*

Nineteen: Lacking; without fruit

> *…And when he had gathered all the people together, there lacked of David's servants nineteen men and Asahel (2 Samuel 2:30 KJV).*

Twenty: The number ten means a trial or testing. For multiples of ten, such as twenty, thirty, forty, etc., begin with a trial or time of testing and combine the symbolic meaning of the first number, such as two for the number twenty. Example: twenty means a trial or time of testing to prove if you have separated the holy from the unholy in your life or circumstances.

> *For twenty years I have been with you, caring for your flocks. In all that time your sheep and goats never miscarried. In all those years I never used a single ram of yours for food (Genesis 31:38 NLT).*

Thirty: A trial or test to prove if you are obedient or conforming to the image to which you have been called.

> *He was thirty years old when he [Joseph] began serving in the court of Pharaoh, the king of Egypt. And when Joseph left Pharaoh's presence, he inspected the entire land of Egypt (Genesis 41:46 NLT).*

Forty: A trial or test to prove if you are ready to rule and reign. Examples: Jesus fasted forty days before being tempted by the devil; the floodwaters rose for forty days and nights; the Israelites wandered for forty years.

Fifty: A trial or test to prove if you are ready to multiply or have abundance; freedom; jubilee; debts paid

> *Set this year apart as holy, a time to proclaim freedom throughout the land… It will be a jubilee year… you may return to the land that belonged to your ancestors … This fiftieth year will be a jubilee… you must not plant your fields or store any of the crops or grapes that grew on their own (Leviticus 25:10-11 NLT).*

Hundred: Plenty; paid in full; fullness

> *Then Isaac sowed in that land and received in that same year a hundredfold; and the LORD blessed him (Genesis 26:12 KJV).*

Thousand: Full maturity

> *I took the wise and respected men you had selected from your tribes and appointed them to serve as judges and officials over you. Some were responsible for a thousand people, some for a hundred, some for fifty, and some for ten (Deuteronomy 1:15 NLT).*

COLORS

Beige: Can symbolize purity (fine linen) but usually means lifeless because it's "without color"

Black: Death; evil; sin; mourning; drought; grief; famine; demonic. A person dressed in black usually represents the demonic. I've never seen black in a dream or vision to symbolize a positive meaning.

> *Weep like a bride dressed in black, mourning the death of her husband (Joel 1:8 NLT).*

Blue: Heaven; things of the Spirit. *Light blue* can represent the demonic since the enemy is in the 2nd heaven, but it can also point to the divine. *Navy Blue* (mix of black and blue) represents *something that looks like God but isn't*, like a familiar spirit. *Royal blue* can mean things of the heavens but can also symbolize divination or demonic. *Dull medium blue* denotes mediocrity in one's heart.

> *There they saw the God of Israel. Under his feet there seemed to be a surface of brilliant sapphire, as clear as the sky itself (Exodus 24:10 NLT).*
>
> *They bring beaten sheets of silver from Tarshish and gold from Uphaz, and they give these materials to skillful craftsmen who make their idols. Then they dress these gods in royal blue and purple robes made by expert tailors (Jeremiah 10:9 NLT).*
>
> *…The riders wore armor that was fiery red and dark blue and yellow. The horses had heads like lions, and fire and smoke and burning sulfur billowed from their mouths. One-third of all the people on earth were killed by these three plagues (Revelation 9:17-18 NLT).*

Brass: Man's ways; something that looks like God (gold) but isn't; refined through fiery trials

> *Because I know how stubborn you were; your neck muscles were iron, your forehead was bronze (Isaiah 48:4 NIV).*

> *And his feet like unto fine brass, as if they burned in a furnace; and his voice as the sound of many waters (Revelation 1:15 KJV).*

Brown: Death; dying; no life

> *The waters of Nimrin are dried up [so the brown bottom can be seen] and the grass is withered...nothing green is left (Isaiah 15:6 NIV).*

Gold: Glory of God; wealth; divinity; wisdom; idolatry

> *And Abram was very rich in cattle, in, silver, and in gold (Genesis 13:2 KJV).*

> *Wisdom is more valuable than gold and crystal. It cannot be purchased with jewels mounted in fine gold (Job 28:17 NLT).*

> *Their idols are merely things of silver and gold, shaped by human hands (Psalms 115:4 NLT).*

> *The silver is mine, and the gold is mine, says the LORD of Heaven's Armies (Haggai 2:8 NLT).*

Green: *Grass green* or *evergreen* means life. *Neon or pale green* can symbolize death or demonic.

> *And I have given every green plant as food for all the wild animals, the birds in the sky, and the small animals that scurry along the ground—everything that has life (Genesis 1:30 NLT).*

> *They set up sacred pillars and Asherah poles at the top of every*

hill and under every green tree (2 Kings 17:10 NLT).

I looked up and saw a horse whose color was pale green. Its rider was named Death (Revelation 6:8 NLT).

Orange: Caution; dangerous

The wild gourd of 2 Kings 4:39 which one of the sons of the prophets gathered ignorantly, supposing them to be good for food, is a poisonous gourd...which resembles a fruit the color and size of an orange... –Smith's Bible Dictionary

Pink: *Light (baby) pink* means innocent whereas *hot pink* symbolizes sexuality or lust.

Purple: Authority; royalty; presence of God

The seat of King Solomon's chair was made of purple fabric, according to Song of Solomon 3:10.

The soldiers twisted together a crown of thorns and put it on his head. They clothed him in a purple robe (John 19:2 NIV).

Red: Blood; life; salvation; control; anger; pride. If a person is wearing a *red shirt*, it indicates the blood of Jesus and it's possible they are representing the Lord in the dream. *Red Hair, shirt, shoes, or clothes* – anger or control. *Red car* – can represent Jesus' blood or pride or anger. *Dark red* – one has grown weary in well doing; the blood of Jesus has become old to them.

Who is this who comes from Edom, from the city of Bozrah, with his clothing stained red? It is I, the LORD, who has the power to save!" (Isaiah 63:1 NLT)

Silver: Redemption; a price has been paid; revelation; idolatry; knowledge

*And he said to Sarah, "Look, I am giving your brother
1,000 pieces of silver in the presence of all these witnesses.
This is to compensate you for any wrong I may have done
to you. This will settle any claim against me, and your
reputation is cleared" (Genesis 20:16 NLT).*

*Give the silver to Aaron and his sons as the redemption price
for the extra firstborn sons (Numbers 3:48 NLT).*

*You must burn their idols in fire, and you must not covet
the silver or gold that covers them. You must not take it
or it will become a trap to you, for it is detestable to the
LORD your God (Deuteronomy 7:25 NLT).*

Teal: Strength; steadfastness; leadership

...As a teil tree, and as an oak... (Isaiah 6:13 KJV).

White: Purity; righteousness; good deeds. However, a person dressed
in white doing bad things or negative symbols in the dream often
symbolizes a religious spirit.

*She [the bride of Christ] has been given the finest of pure
white linen to wear. For the fine linen represents the good
deeds of God's holy people (Revelation 19:8 NLT).*

*...Even Satan disguises himself as an angel of light (2
Corinthians 11:14 NLT).*

Yellow: Yellow usually symbolizes *fear*. It is slang for coward or fearful.

MISCELLANEOUS

Actor: Pretending; see *Celebrity*

Airplane: Powerful ministry or anointing; way to escape; exercising faith

Alcohol: Intoxicating; drugged by demonic thoughts or actions; tired; spiritually asleep; see *Wine*

Aliens: Christians; demons; foreign, unusual thinking; fear

Ambulance: Emergency situation or one viewed as emergency, therefore an over-reaction; emotional drama; needing emotional, physical or spiritual rescue

Angels: Spiritual beings, holy or unholy. Look for other positive or negative things the angels or others are doing in the dream.

Ants: Busy work; Church; powerless; pestilence; annoyance; *Ant bites* –irritation; tormenting thoughts; biting words

Apartment: Temporary "place," meaning a different way of handling situations than one normally does; see *Home*.

Aquarium: Church; family; being in a *fish tank* meaning *without privacy*; totally exposed

Ashes: Past trauma; old thought or circumstances; need for inner healing or forgiveness

Asian people: Hard workers; overly hard work

Assassination: "Killing" someone by thoughts, words or actions; see *Death*

Attic: Spiritual or other thoughts; going to a "high place" in the Spirit; see *Cellar*

Attorney: Religious spirit; legalism; advocate; accuser

Baby: New thought; new idea; new relationship, whether good or evil

Back: Unclear; *looking at one's own back* means the future is not yet clear

Back door: The past; taking a less-than-honest way out of a situation (also side door)

Back yard: See *Back Door*

Baggage: Emotional baggage; unforgiveness; need for inner healing; past trauma

Baseball: See *Sports*

Basement: See *Cellar*

Basketball: See *Sports*

Bathroom: Place of cleansing, repentance. *Urinating* – angry (pissed off); *Pooping* – getting rid of sin; repentance; talking too much (diarrhea of the mouth); *Toilet not flushing* – not thoroughly repenting or dealing with a situation; *Shower/Tub* – place of cleansing; repentance

Battery: Energy; tiredness; exhaustion; anointing

Beach: Ministry field; the world; works of the flesh

Bed: Intimate agreement with someone or an idea (in bed with); rest; covenant (good or evil)

Bedtime: Putting an issue "to bed," meaning to finish the situation the dream is addressing; *Going to bed* has the same meaning.

Bee: Busy; busybody; gossip; hard worker; destroyer; stinging words

Bell: Warning; alarm; ending; beginning

Belt: Truth; constraining; judgment; punishment

Bicycle: Works of the flesh because you must pedal to keep it going, rather than a vehicle like an airplane or sailboat that can represent faith; *see Boat*

Birds: Demons; angels; messengers; gossip; see *Colors*

Blanket: Covering; hidden motives; see *Comforter*

Bleeding: Emotional wounding; offended

Blue collar: Average worker or working conditions, not an executive

Blueprints: Plans (of the Lord or the enemy)

Boat: Faith; Church or church group; anointing; see *Bicycle*

Boots: Warring in the spirit, getting through a "muddy" or unclear, difficult situation

Box: Legalism; religious spirit; control; feeling you are being controlled, whether true or not

Brick: Stronghold (mindset that doesn't align with godly thinking); difficult problem to solve or one incorrectly viewed as such ("It hit me like a brick."); harsh words

Bride: Natural marriage; thinking you are to be married, whether correct thinking or not; coming into intimate agreement with an idea, whether godly or demonic

Bridge: Place of transition; joining of thoughts, ideas, people

Briefcase: Natural work; situation that occurred and was over quickly; spiritual gifts

Brother: See *Sister*

Bull: Anger; rage; control; pushing to have one's way; prosperity (bull market)

Bus: Group of people with common purpose; Church or church group

Butterfly: Freedom; moving quickly from one thought or idea to another

Cabin: Temporary place; refuge; retreat; see *Apartment*

Cabinet: Hidden motives; unforgiveness; matters put away for a long time; inner healing need

Cafeteria: Place of "eating," partaking of spiritual food; Church or other group

Cake: Fellowship; sweet; easy (piece of cake); *Birthday cake* – aging; viewing oneself or others as old

Cancer: Situation "eating" at you; *Breast Cancer* – situation disturbing your heart, meaning your emotions

Car: Vehicle for transporting the anointing; person; life; ministry; *Car wreck* – argument between people; *Driver* – one in control; *Passenger* – not in control in a situation

Cards: Playing emotional games; truth (laying your cards on the table)

Cat: Self-pity; independence; insulting (catty); sulking; see *Pet*

Cave: Hiding; escape; time of withdrawing to find the Lord's purposes or direction

Celebrity: Consider what they would symbolically mean in the movies or TV programs in which you've seen them. For example, if you dream of Monica in *Friends*, she could symbolize a part of you that is overly organized or competitive; see *Actor.*

Cellar: Old issues not yet dealt with; unforgiveness; base motives

Cell phone: Communication; spirit calling out to you (good or evil)

CEO: The one in control, for example a good or bad spirit or attitude; controlling spirit; one's boss; spouse

Chair: Authority; rest

Check: Faith; see *Money*

Chewing: Meditating; "chewing" on an idea or thought

Chicken: Fear

Children: Young in the spirit; immature; students; congregation; *One's own children* often mean what they symbolize to you. For example, my grown children symbolize what they have recently gone through in their own life, when I find myself dealing with similar issues.

Christmas: Spiritual gifts; Christmas season

Church: Group of people with a common purpose; Church or church group

Closet: Hidden motives; need for inner healing; secret sin

Clothes: Attitudes; condition of one's heart; see *Colors, Shirt, Pants, Dress, Skirts*

Clouds: Positive or negative signs; depression; discouragement; bad news

Coast-guard cutter: Anointing to cut through hard or cold situations

Coat: Prophetic mantle; five-fold ministry; career

Coffee: Fellowship; bitterness; sharing a similar point-of-view

Coins: See *Money, Purse, Treasure*

Comforter: Holy Spirit

Computer: Information; news; prophetic word; thoughts; issues one is "processing"

Convertible: Pride; exposed; self-righteous

Couch: Lazy (couch potato); rest; relaxation

Crossroads: Decision; critical juncture

Cruise ship: Church or church group; see *Boat*

Curtains: Hidden (if closed); revelation (if open)

Dark: Unclear; hidden; not yet revealed; evil; sin; see *Light*

Daughter: See *Children*

Death: Ending; words, actions or thoughts that "killed" a part of you or another; sorrow. If you dream of someone who is deceased, they probably represent what they meant when alive. However, if the deceased person is dead *in the dream*, yet they are speaking, it could also indicate "dead words." These are words spoken by another person, or even prophetic words that brought death rather than life.

Deer: Someone dear to you; attitude or point-of-view that you hold dear; one following the Lord

Den: Casual place; family; heart of a matter; hiding place

Denim: Because the fabric is medium blue in color, it can mean mediocrity of one's heart toward the Lord or a situation; since it is heavyweight and blue, it can indicate depression; casual.

Desk: Spiritual office; natural work; ministry

Diamonds: Treasure; precious; eternal value

Doctor: Healer; Jesus; pastor or other leader

Dog: If it's your own sweet dog, it can mean an aspect of the Holy Spirit (one who is loyal and closer than a brother). If it's a mean dog or one you don't know, it means a demonic or unclean spirit.

Door: Opportunity; new opening; *Double-doors* symbolize two opportunities that often work together

Dove: Holy Spirit; peace; promise; new life; life

Dragon: See *Snake*

Dress: Grace; righteousness; see *Color*

Drowning: Emotionally overwhelmed; debt; grief

Drugs: Attitude or thought caused by agreement with ungodly thinking; see *Alcohol*

Drunk: Entertaining ungodly thoughts, motives, attitudes; see *Drugs*

Duck: Easy target

Dust, Dirt: Flesh; *Dry cracked ground* symbolizes a place in one's heart where life once was and now is totally barren; see *Mud*

Eagle: Prophetic; clear vision; powerful anointing

Earrings: Bondage (to the Lord or evil); hearing; vanity

Earthquake: Crisis; trauma; one's foundation is shaking; financial chaos; shocking events; spiritual chaos

East: Beginning; see *Sunrise*

Eating: Participating; believing; faith

Egg: Promise of new life; new attitude; new plans

Elephant: Memory; huge task (Mowing my lawn is like eating an elephant.); ignoring the obvious (the elephant in the room)

Elevator: If going up, symbolizes going to a "higher place" in the Spirit, one's thoughts or decisions; going down represents going to a "lower place" such as depression or backsliding

Ex-husband or Ex-wife: One's "old man;" see *Old man*

Face: Identity; emotional or spiritual condition

Falling: In a backslidden condition; depression; loss of emotional or other support

Father: God; apostle; pastor; one's own father; *Father-in-law* – legalism, could represent a natural father-in-law

Fatter/Thinner: Weight symbolizes a person is more, or less, important in the dreamer's point-of-view than they usually are; weight gain; weight loss

Fear: Spirit of fear; fear of a specific issue

Feet: Peace; walk with the Lord

Fence: Boundary; legalism; obstacle

Field: Harvest field; ministry

Fingers: Tools of war; five-fold ministry; judgment

Fire: Fire of God; testing; anointing; rage

Fireplace: Heated discussion or situation; anger

Fire station: Church; place of trial or testing; rescue from argument or anger

Fish: The Lord; believer; humanity; *Fishing* – evangelism; ministry; nosy

Flies: Lies; nuisance; unclean; gossip

Flip-flops: Changing one's mind; indecisive

Flood: See *Drowning*

Floor: Foundational truth; bottom line; basis; lowly; motive

Flowers: Romance; sweet, flowery words; flattery

Flying: Faith; easy escape; fantasy; bird's-eye view of a situation; see *Power lines*

Fog: Clouded thoughts; obscure vision; see *Clouds*

Football: See *Sports*

Forest: Loss of direction; obscure vision; leadership

Foundation: See *Floor*

France or French people: Romance

Friend: Ask yourself what a particular friend means to you symbolically; Holy Spirit; the Lord; see *Children*

Frog: Sickness; unclean spirit

Front door: The future; decision you are about to make

Fruit: Fruits of the Holy Spirit; positive or negative results of an action or inaction

Funeral: See *Death*

Funnel cloud: See *Tornado*

Garage: Hidden motives; thoughts, issues, or attitudes one isn't dealing with (stored away); need for inner healing or forgiveness

Garbage: Repentance; deliverance; demonic; emotional baggage; judgment

Garden: Secret place with the Lord; ministry; career; one's life; one's heart

Gasoline: Strife; contention; anger; gossip

Gate: Blockage; entrance

Germany or German people: Strict; stern; without grace

Ghost: Need for inner healing or forgiveness of past issues; fear

Gift: Spiritual gift; natural gift

Goat: Unbeliever; rebellious; cruelty; brutality; demonic; unfairly blamed (scapegoat)

Golf: See *Sports*

Grandmother: Inheritance; past; need for inner healing; *Grandchild –* natural grandchild; heir; inheritance, including one's destiny or God's plan; see *Children; Mother*

Gun: Power; powerlessness (gun that doesn't fire or fires slowly); words; words of accusation; prayer; faith; faithlessness

Hair: One's *glory*, or perceived righteousness; way of thinking; *Red hair – anger; Golden hair –* righteousness, God's glory; *Beautiful hair –* righteousness; *Dark blonde hair –* looks like God's glory but isn't; man's ways; *Hair falling out –* one has done something to lessen their glory; *Silver hair –* wisdom; *Shaved head –* shame; humiliation

Hallway: Transition; see *Bridge*

Hammer: Preaching; judgment; truth; lacking grace

Hat: Way of thinking: point of view; mindset; attitude; career; responsibilities

Head: Authority; husband; way of thinking; mindset; pastor; covering; boss

Heavy machinery: Powerful anointing or ministry; powerful spirit for or against you

Highway: Spiritual path; direction one is taking regarding a life choice or decision

Holding hands: In agreement with a person, thought, idea, attitude, etc.

Hole in the ground: Depression; discouragement; negative attitude or thoughts; fear

Hometown: Doing things the way one did things at the time of living in that location; inner-healing need

Homosexual: Love of things like oneself; narcissism; acts against nature including abuse by leadership; homosexual behavior

Honey: Enlightenment; revelation; sweetness; anointing

Horse: War; judgment; righteousness; movement of the Spirit; see *Color*

Hospital: Place of healing; hope; church; ministry

Hotel: Temporary place; literal hotel; business; travel

House: One's own life issues; if one dreams of being in their own home, the dream is addressing their own heart; if the dream takes place in another's home, it is likely addressing something you are doing that you have in common with that person

Hurricane: See *Tornado*

Husband: A spirit, thought or attitude, etc. to which you are "married," or in intimate agreement; the Lord; can be one's natural husband (likely doesn't represent a future one); see *Children, Mother*

Ice: Cold, hard words or attitude; deliberate coldness or disregard

Ice cream: Easy, sweet "palatable" words spoken in faith (milk of the Word); harsh message given in a soft way

Indian: Flesh; anger; war-like; primitive nature

Insurance: Protection; faith; salvation

Intersection: See *Crossroads*

Ironing: Working through difficulties; repenting from sin; reconciliation

Italy or Italian people: Romance; family; food

Jacket: See *Coat*

Jewelry: Spiritual gifts; pride; treasures

Jews: Legalism; religious spirit; without grace

Judge: See *Lawyer*

Key: Authority; power; knowledge

Killing: See *Assassination* and *Death*

Kiss: Intimate agreement with a person, thought, idea

Kitchen: Heart of a matter; one's heart; scheming, meaning something is "cooked up"

Knee: Submission; obedience to the Lord or another

Knife: Cutting words or actions; Word of God; see *Sword*

Ladder: Going to a "higher place;" spiritual thoughts; on the path to one's destiny; see *Elevator*

Lake: Life; pollution (Lack of free-flowing water); see *River*; stagnant or small thinking; place where once the Spirit flowed freely but now is constrained; see *Aquarium*

Lamb: Innocence; kindness; the Lord

Lamp: Revelation; clear; obvious; the Lord; see *Light*

Laundry: Drama; chaos; sin; repentance; need for inner healing; see *Baggage*

Lawyer: See *Attorney*

Leaves: Hiding; death of a situation or relationship

Left: Usually indicates a spiritually negative situation or demonic intrusion

Legs: Strength; balance; support

Light: Revelation; knowledge; righteousness; see *Dark*

Living room: Situations happening in your current life

Lizard: See *Snake*

Lunchroom: Church; place where one "eats" or gets their spiritual food

Makeup: Deception; hidden motives or intentions; pretense; insecurity; vanity; reconciliation

Man: See *Woman*

Married: In full agreement with a thought, attitude, idea

Masturbation: Narcissism; love of oneself; self-gratification; see *Sex*

Meat: Deeper doctrines of the faith

Mechanic: The Lord; spiritual counselor, including pastor, prophet, home group or other leader; a need for repair of one's theology, point-of-view, attitude or heart condition

Milk: Basic gospel message

Mirror: Vanity; self-love; identity; reflection; introspection; narcissism

Mobile home: Temporary place, meaning a temporary point-of-view

Money: Identity; anointing; faith (the currency of the Kingdom)

Moon: Church (reflection of the Lord, the Sun); wife; occult

Mother: Church; source; one's job, because it is their financial source; one's natural mother; origin or source of a thought or idea. When I dream of my own mother, she symbolizes the most mature part of me; at times she can mean I'm dealing with fear because she did. Think about the issues with which your mother struggles as you consider your dream's meaning.

Mother-in-law: Legalism (law); whatever she represents to you in real life

Motorcycle: Exposed; pride, because they are uncovered; independence (vehicle for one)

Mountain: Kingdom; sector of society; seemingly insurmountable obstacle

Movie: Memories from the past; reliving or continuing to think on old issues; unforgiveness

Moving: Changing ways of thinking, attitudes, actions or reactions (whether from good to bad or vice-versa); natural moving

Mud: Flesh; shame; bad name; abusive or malicious remarks; slander; stuck in a situation; see *Dust*

Mumbling: Familiar spirit (they "mutter and peep"); unclear or indistinct motives or actions

Naked: Fully exposed; self-righteousness; vulnerable

NASA: See *Aliens*

Neck: Haughty; stubborn; strong-willed

Newspaper: News; prophetic or foretelling; gossip

New York City: Liberty (Statue of Liberty); freedom; sophisticated; economy

Noise: Interference; annoying situation preventing one from hearing God clearly

North: Judgment

Nose: Discernment; busybody; meddling

Oak Tree: Strength; long-suffering; leadership

Ocean: See *Beach*

Office: Five-fold ministry; work

Oil: Anointing; unity; spiritual gifts

Old Man: One's "old man," meaning the old nature that must be crucified; if the old man has silver hair, can mean *wisdom.*

Oven: Hidden motives; unforgiveness; seething anger; inner-healing need; see *Kitchen*

Owl: Wisdom; occult; vision in difficult circumstances

Pants: Authority ("wearing the pants"); control

Pastor: The Lord; five-fold ministry; leading of the Lord; covering; leader; legalism; whatever the particular pastor symbolizes to you

Path: Walk with God; decision (whether good or bad)

Pets: Best friend; one's own precious pet can represent the Holy Spirit; see *Dog;* see *Cat*

Picture: See *Movie*

Polar bear: Destroyer; hard, cutting words; deliberate coldness or disregard

Police: Natural or spiritual authority; Jesus; legalism; enforcer of a curse; protector

Pond: See *Lake*

Pool: Family (gene pool); church family; work or other group

Potatoes: Root motives; see *Cellar*

Power lines: Dangerous situation; crossing spiritual or natural boundaries

Pregnancy: New idea on which one is working or considering; *labor pains* – working through trials

President: See *CEO*

Purse: Identity; treasure; heart of a matter

Rain: Revival; blessing; trial; depression; discouragement; iniquity; blessings; abundance

Rainbow: Promise; end of a trial; new beginning

Rapture: Spiritual newness; warning

Refrigerator: Heart; hidden motives; need for inner healing; stored away memories

Right: Natural circumstances; belief one is doing the right thing; can mean a good or right point-of-view

Ring: Authority; permission; coming into agreement

River: Prophetic flow; life; ways of God

Rock: The Lord; stability; accusation

Rocket: Sudden change; powerful progress; ministry

Roller Coaster: Emotional or spiritual ups-and-downs

Roof: Covering; Church; husband; job; relationship with the Lord; announcement (shout it from the rooftops)

Rooms: Five-fold ministry; thought or idea; see *Living Room, Den, Garage, Hallway, Bathroom, Bedroom, Kitchen*

Roots: Motives; hidden cause of issues

Rose: Love; beauty; romance; see *Colors*

Running: On a fast track, either good or bad; *hard to run* – powerlessness; lack of faith; depression

Rut: Stuck in a situation; path to follow

Sailboat: Faith; see *Boat*

Salt: Covenant; seasoning; ministry; preservation

Sand: Shifting foundation; poor decision; ungodly motives; instability

Scarf: See *Neck*

School: Church; attitude or situation of learning something new

Scream: Fear; calling for help

Sea: Humanity; evangelism; See *Beach*

Seeds: Words; faith; iniquity

Sewing: Reconciliation; joining together; counseling; mending

Sex: Intimate agreement; agreement with a wrong idea, person, motive, or attitude

Shelf: Not dealing with a situation; an old idea or plan; need for inner healing; unforgiveness

Ship: See *Boat* and *Cruise ship*

Shirt: Clothing worn over one's heart, so the color denotes one's attitude or motive; see *Clothes;* see particular *Color* of shirt; *Striped shirt* – indicates healing, particularly if red-and-white or green-and-white stripes (By His stripes we were healed); *No shirt* – not seeing the need for covering, therefore self-righteous; exposed; shame

Shoes: Walk with the Lord; see *Boots*

Shopping: Considering "buying into" a particular line of thinking or idea

Sister: Natural sister; female believer in Christ; one in agreement; see *Children*

Ski: See *Sports*

Skirt: Grace; righteousness; see *Color*

Sleep: Unaware; laziness; not on the path in one's walk with God

Slide: See *Falling*

Smoke: Deception; delusion; hidden motives or actions; *Smoking* – anger, lingering anger

Smoking: Anger; offense; unforgiveness

Snake: Demonic; see *Color; White Snake* – religious spirit; *Yellow Snake* – spirit of fear; *Python* – divination; *Rattlesnake* – anger, meanness ("mean as a rattlesnake"); *Snake with a man's face* – fear of man; man-pleasing spirit; dysfunctional need for man's approval

Snow: Grace; purity; see *Ice Cream*

Soldier: Spiritual warfare; angel; demon

Son: Offspring; see *Children*

South: Negative turn of events (things are "headed south")

Spider: Deception; lies; entrapment

Sports: "Taking the land" for the Lord (especially golf, baseball, soccer, football because they are played on land); overcoming; inheritance; ministry; jest; diversion; mockery, ridicule; taking a position on a matter

Square: Legalism; hard words; harsh point-of-view; outdated thinking

Stairway: Spiritual progress; going to a higher place

Stars: Children; God's children; five-fold ministry

Stone: Witness; see *Rock*

Stop sign or red light: See *Traffic Signs*

Storage unit: Place where emotions are stored; inner healing; unforgiveness

Storm: Argument; crisis; emotional turmoil

Stripes: Healing; see *Shirt*

Submarine: Hidden motives or emotions; repressed emotions such as anger or offense

Subway: See *Submarine*

Sugar: See *Honey*

Suitcase: Emotional baggage; past experiences; unforgiveness; see *Baggage*

Sulfur: Demonic; destruction

Sun: The Lord; husband; center of one's universe

Sunrise: New beginning; new idea or way of thinking

Sunset: Ending; end of a relationship, job, or other situation; death

Sweater or sweat clothes: Heavy emotions; depression; bothersome or worrisome situation (makes one sweat); works of the flesh

Sweeping: Repentance; deliverance; ministry

Swimming pool: See *Pool*

Sword: Word of God; harsh, cutting words

Table: "Place" of meeting or agreement; showing your thoughts or idea clearly (laying cards on the table); put an issue aside for a future time (table an idea)

Tea: Refreshing; fellowship

Tears: Compassion; emotion; sadness; precious

Teeth: Wisdom (as in wisdom teeth); *Teeth falling out* – lack of wisdom; one has done something regretful; see *Chewing*

Telephone: See *Cell Phone*

Television: Memories; need for inner healing; message; prophecy; news

Tennis: See *Sports*

Tennis shoes: See *Running*

Thorns: Cares of life; demonic; disease; gossip; unforgiveness; curse; persecution

Thunder: Warning; God's judgment; impending conflict

Tie: See *Neck*

Tools: Spiritual gifts; skills

Tornado: Iniquity (doing those things one doesn't want to do yet seems unable to control); emotional upheaval; intense argument

Traffic Signs: *Stop sign or red light* – one should stop their current actions; one feels they should stop an action, whether correct in this position or not; *Green light* indicates one should pursue what is in their heart, though also could show one's heart rather than the Lord's will

Train: Church (large vehicle carrying many people to a common "place"); ministry

Tree: Leadership; humanity; *Tree trunk* – main body of a person, life, idea; *Roots* – motives; foundational cause of a situation; *Tree stump* – hope for restoration

Trip: On the wrong path; negative change in one's point-of-view or attitude (She tripped and got drunk again.)

Truck: See *Car* and *Heavy Machinery*

Tsunami: See *Flood*

Undertow: See *Flood*

Underwear: Exposed

Vacuum Cleaner: See *Sweeping*

Van: See *Bus*

Walking: On (or off) the path toward the Lord's will; going through life's circumstances

Water: Anointing; Word of God; cleansing from sin; see *Ocean, River, Lake*

Wedding dress: Natural wedding; becoming intimate with a spirit, thought or attitude whether good or bad; one thinking they are to be married, whether true or not

Weeds: Sin; works of the flesh; cares of life

Wife: Spirit to whom one is married; natural wife; see *Children*

Wind: Holy Spirit; God's ways; demonic

Windows: Opportunity; way of escape; revelation; see *Curtains*

Wine: Anointing; spiritual gifts; mocking; irrational actions

Witch: Witchcraft; manipulation; seduction; rebellion

Woman: If the woman is unknown, notice the details: What are her actions? Is her hair a certain color? See *Hair*. What color are her clothes? See *Clothes* and *Color*.

Wood: Humanity; stubbornness

Working: Natural work; ministry

X-Ray: Exposing hidden motives; inner healing

Young: New life; renewed vigor and energy; immature

Dream Interpretation
Tools

e-Newsletter
Learn more about how to interpret your dreams.

Seminars
With a passion to see others healed, Sylvia has activated congregations, in various denominations across the U.S. and other nations, to hear God's voice prophetically and to interpret their dreams.

Webinars
Coming soon, look for online webinar and video reources to help you learn to interpret your dreams.

www.DreamInterpretationToolkit.com

 Facebook.com/DreamInterpretationToolkit